Nutshell Series
Hornbook Series
and
Black Letter Series
of
WEST PUBLISHING COMPANY
P.O. Box 64526
St. Paul, Minnesota 55164–0526

Accounting
FARIS' ACCOUNTING AND LAW IN A NUTSHELL, 377 pages, 1984. Softcover. (Text)

Administrative Law
GELLHORN AND LEVIN'S ADMINISTRATIVE LAW AND PROCESS IN A NUTSHELL, Third Edition, 479 pages, 1990. Softcover. (Text)

Admiralty
MARAIST'S ADMIRALTY IN A NUTSHELL, Second Edition, 379 pages, 1988. Softcover. (Text)

SCHOENBAUM'S HORNBOOK ON ADMIRALTY AND MARITIME LAW, Student Edition, 692 pages, 1987 with 1989 pocket part. (Text)

Agency—Partnership
REUSCHLEIN AND GREGORY'S HORNBOOK ON THE LAW OF AGENCY AND PARTNERSHIP, Second Edition, 683 pages, 1990. (Text)

STEFFEN'S AGENCY-PARTNERSHIP IN A NUTSHELL, 364 pages, 1977. Softcover. (Text)

American Indian Law
CANBY'S AMERICAN INDIAN LAW IN A NUTSHELL, Second Edition, 336 pages, 1988. Softcover. (Text)

Antitrust—see also Regulated Industries, Trade Regulation

GELLHORN'S ANTITRUST LAW AND ECONOMICS IN A NUTSHELL, Third Edition, 472 pages,

Antitrust—Continued

1986. Softcover. (Text)

HOVENKAMP'S BLACK LETTER ON ANTITRUST, 323 pages, 1986. Softcover. (Review)

HOVENKAMP'S HORNBOOK ON ECONOMICS AND FEDERAL ANTITRUST LAW, Student Edition, 414 pages, 1985. (Text)

SULLIVAN'S HORNBOOK OF THE LAW OF ANTITRUST, 886 pages, 1977. (Text)

Appellate Advocacy—see Trial and Appellate Advocacy

Art Law

DUBOFF'S ART LAW IN A NUTSHELL, 335 pages, 1984. Softcover. (Text)

Banking Law

BANKING LAW: SELECTED STATUTES AND REGULATIONS. Softcover. 263 pages, 1991.

LOVETT'S BANKING AND FINANCIAL INSTITUTIONS LAW IN A NUTSHELL, Second Edition, 464 pages, 1988. Softcover. (Text)

Civil Procedure—see also Federal Jurisdiction and Procedure

CLERMONT'S BLACK LETTER ON CIVIL PROCEDURE, Second Edition, 332 pages, 1988. Softcover. (Review)

FRIEDENTHAL, KANE AND MILLER'S HORNBOOK ON CIVIL PROCEDURE, 876 pages, 1985. (Text)

KANE'S CIVIL PROCEDURE IN A NUTSHELL, Third Edition, 303 pages, 1991. Softcover. (Text)

KOFFLER AND REPPY'S HORNBOOK ON COMMON LAW PLEADING, 663 pages, 1969. (Text)

SIEGEL'S HORNBOOK ON NEW YORK PRACTICE, Second Edition, Student Edition, 1068 pages, 1991. Softcover. (Text)

Commercial Law

BAILEY AND HAGEDORN'S SECURED TRANSACTIONS IN A NUTSHELL, Third Edition, 390 pages, 1988. Softcover. (Text)

HENSON'S HORNBOOK ON SECURED TRANSACTIONS UNDER THE U.C.C., Second Edition, 504 pages, 1979, with 1979 pocket part. (Text)

NICKLES' BLACK LETTER ON COMMERCIAL PAPER, 450 pages, 1988. Softcover. (Review)

SPEIDEL'S BLACK LETTER ON SALES AND SALES FINANCING, 363 pages, 1984. Softcover. (Review)

STOCKTON'S SALES IN A NUT-

Commercial Law—Continued

SHELL, Second Edition, 370 pages, 1981. Softcover. (Text)

STONE'S UNIFORM COMMERCIAL CODE IN A NUTSHELL, Third Edition, 580 pages, 1989. Softcover. (Text)

WEBER AND SPEIDEL'S COMMERCIAL PAPER IN A NUTSHELL, Third Edition, 404 pages, 1982. Softcover. (Text)

WHITE AND SUMMERS' HORNBOOK ON THE UNIFORM COMMERCIAL CODE, Third Edition, Student Edition, 1386 pages, 1988. (Text)

Community Property

MENNELL AND BOYKOFF'S COMMUNITY PROPERTY IN A NUTSHELL, Second Edition, 432 pages, 1988. Softcover. (Text)

Comparative Law

GLENDON, GORDON AND OSAKWE'S COMPARATIVE LEGAL TRADITIONS IN A NUTSHELL. 402 pages, 1982. Softcover. (Text)

Conflict of Laws

HAY'S BLACK LETTER ON CONFLICT OF LAWS, 330 pages, 1989. Softcover. (Review)

SCOLES AND HAY'S HORNBOOK ON CONFLICT OF LAWS, Student Edition, approximately 1100 pages, November 1991 Pub. (Text)

SIEGEL'S CONFLICTS IN A NUTSHELL, 470 pages, 1982. Softcover. (Text)

Constitutional Law—Civil Rights

BARRON AND DIENES' BLACK LETTER ON CONSTITUTIONAL LAW, Third Edition, 440 pages, 1991. Softcover. (Review)

BARRON AND DIENES' CONSTITUTIONAL LAW IN A NUTSHELL, Second Edition, 483 pages, 1991. Softcover. (Text)

ENGDAHL'S CONSTITUTIONAL FEDERALISM IN A NUTSHELL, Second Edition, 411 pages, 1987. Softcover. (Text)

MARKS AND COOPER'S STATE CONSTITUTIONAL LAW IN A NUTSHELL, 329 pages, 1988. Softcover. (Text)

NOWAK AND ROTUNDA'S HORNBOOK ON CONSTITUTIONAL LAW, Fourth Edition, approximately 1275 pages, August, 1991 Pub. (Text)

VIEIRA'S CONSTITUTIONAL CIVIL RIGHTS IN A NUTSHELL, Second Edition, 322 pages, 1990. Softcover. (Text)

Constitutional Law—Civil Rights—Continued

WILLIAMS' CONSTITUTIONAL ANALYSIS IN A NUTSHELL, 388 pages, 1979. Softcover. (Text)

Consumer Law—see also Commercial Law

EPSTEIN AND NICKLES' CONSUMER LAW IN A NUTSHELL, Second Edition, 418 pages, 1981. Softcover. (Text)

Contracts

CALAMARI AND PERILLO'S BLACK LETTER ON CONTRACTS, Second Edition, 462 pages, 1990. Softcover. (Review)

CALAMARI AND PERILLO'S HORNBOOK ON CONTRACTS, Third Edition, 1049 pages, 1987. (Text)

CORBIN'S TEXT ON CONTRACTS, One Volume Student Edition, 1224 pages, 1952. (Text)

FRIEDMAN'S CONTRACT REMEDIES IN A NUTSHELL, 323 pages, 1981. Softcover. (Text)

KEYES' GOVERNMENT CONTRACTS IN A NUTSHELL, Second Edition, 557 pages, 1990. Softcover. (Text)

SCHABER AND ROHWER'S CONTRACTS IN A NUTSHELL, Third Edition, 457 pages, 1990. Softcover. (Text)

Copyright—see Patent and Copyright Law

Corporations

HAMILTON'S BLACK LETTER ON CORPORATIONS, Second Edition, 513 pages, 1986. Softcover. (Review)

HAMILTON'S THE LAW OF CORPORATIONS IN A NUTSHELL, Third Edition, 518 pages, 1991. Softcover. (Text)

HENN AND ALEXANDER'S HORNBOOK ON LAWS OF CORPORATIONS, Third Edition, Student Edition, 1371 pages, 1983, with 1986 pocket part. (Text)

Corrections

KRANTZ' THE LAW OF CORRECTIONS AND PRISONERS' RIGHTS IN A NUTSHELL, Third Edition, 407 pages, 1988. Softcover. (Text)

Creditors' Rights

EPSTEIN'S DEBTOR-CREDITOR LAW IN A NUTSHELL, Fourth Edition, 401 pages, 1991. Softcover. (Text)

NICKLES AND EPSTEIN'S BLACK LETTER ON CREDITORS' RIGHTS AND BANKRUPTCY, 576 pages, 1989. (Review)

Environmental Law—Continued

pages, 1988. Softcover. (Text)

RODGERS' HORNBOOK ON ENVIRONMENTAL LAW, 956 pages, 1977, with 1984 pocket part. (Text)

Equity—see Remedies

Estate Planning—see also Trusts and Estates; Taxation—Estate and Gift

LYNN'S AN INTRODUCTION TO ESTATE PLANNING IN A NUTSHELL, Third Edition, 370 pages, 1983. Softcover. (Text)

Evidence

BROUN AND BLAKEY'S BLACK LETTER ON EVIDENCE, 269 pages, 1984. Softcover. (Review)

GRAHAM'S FEDERAL RULES OF EVIDENCE IN A NUTSHELL, Second Edition, 473 pages, 1987. Softcover. (Text)

LILLY'S AN INTRODUCTION TO THE LAW OF EVIDENCE, Second Edition, 585 pages, 1987. (Text)

McCORMICK'S HORNBOOK ON EVIDENCE, Fourth Edition, Student Edition, approximately 1200 pages, January

1992 Pub. (Text)

ROTHSTEIN'S EVIDENCE IN A NUTSHELL: STATE AND FEDERAL RULES, Second Edition, 514 pages, 1981. Softcover. (Text)

Federal Jurisdiction and Procedure

CURRIE'S FEDERAL JURISDICTION IN A NUTSHELL, Third Edition, 242 pages, 1990. Softcover. (Text)

REDISH'S BLACK LETTER ON FEDERAL JURISDICTION, Second Edition, 234 pages, 1991. Softcover. (Review)

WRIGHT'S HORNBOOK ON FEDERAL COURTS, Fourth Edition, Student Edition, 870 pages, 1983. (Text)

First Amendment

Future Interests—see Trusts and Estates

Gender Discrimination—see also Employment Discrimination

THOMAS' SEX DISCRIMINATION IN A NUTSHELL, Second Edition, approximately 400 pages, 1991. Softcover. (Text)

Health Law—see Medicine, Law and

Labor and Employment Law—
Continued

NOLAN'S LABOR ARBITRATION LAW AND PRACTICE IN A NUTSHELL, 358 pages, 1979. Softcover. (Text)

Land Finance—Property Security—see Real Estate Transactions

Land Use

HAGMAN AND JUERGENSMEYER'S HORNBOOK ON URBAN PLANNING AND LAND DEVELOPMENT CONTROL LAW, Second Edition, Student Edition, 680 pages, 1986. (Text)

WRIGHT AND WRIGHT'S LAND USE IN A NUTSHELL, Second Edition, 356 pages, 1985. Softcover. (Text)

Legal Method and Legal System—see also Legal Research, Legal Writing

KEMPIN'S HISTORICAL INTRODUCTION TO ANGLO-AMERICAN LAW IN A NUTSHELL, Third Edition, 323 pages, 1990. Softcover. (Text)

REYNOLDS' JUDICIAL PROCESS IN A NUTSHELL, Second Edition, approximately 310 pages, 1991. Softcover. (Text)

Legal Research

COHEN'S LEGAL RESEARCH IN A NUTSHELL, Fourth Edition, 452 pages, 1985. Softcover. (Text)

COHEN, BERRING AND OLSON'S HOW TO FIND THE LAW, Ninth Edition, 716 pages, 1989. (Text)

Legal Writing and Drafting

SQUIRES AND ROMBAUER'S LEGAL WRITING IN A NUTSHELL, 294 pages, 1982. Softcover. (Text)

Legislation—see also Legal Writing and Drafting

DAVIES' LEGISLATIVE LAW AND PROCESS IN A NUTSHELL, Second Edition, 346 pages, 1986. Softcover. (Text)

Local Government

MCCARTHY'S LOCAL GOVERNMENT LAW IN A NUTSHELL, Third Edition, 435 pages, 1990. Softcover. (Text)

REYNOLDS' HORNBOOK ON LOCAL GOVERNMENT LAW, 860 pages, 1982, with 1990 pocket part. (Text)

Mass Communication Law

ZUCKMAN, GAYNES, CARTER AND DEE'S MASS COMMUNICATIONS LAW IN A NUTSHELL, Third Edition, 538 pages, 1988. Softcover. (Text)

Medicine, Law and

HALL AND ELLMAN'S HEALTH CARE LAW AND ETHICS IN A NUTSHELL, 401 pages, 1990. Softcover (Text)

JARVIS, CLOSEN, HERMANN AND LEONARD'S AIDS LAW IN A NUTSHELL, 349 pages, 1991. Softcover. (Text)

KING'S THE LAW OF MEDICAL MALPRACTICE IN A NUTSHELL, Second Edition, 342 pages, 1986. Softcover. (Text)

Military Law

SHANOR AND TERRELL'S MILITARY LAW IN A NUTSHELL, 378 pages, 1980. Softcover. (Text)

Mortgages—see Real Estate Transactions

Natural Resources Law—see Energy and Natural Resources Law, Environmental Law

Office Practice—see also Computers and Law, Interviewing and Counseling, Negotiation

HEGLAND'S TRIAL AND PRACTICE SKILLS IN A NUTSHELL, 346 pages, 1978. Softcover (Text)

Oil and Gas—see also Energy and Natural Resources Law

HEMINGWAY'S HORNBOOK ON THE LAW OF OIL AND GAS, Third Edition, Student Edition, approximately 700 pages, Aug., 1991 Pub. (Text)

LOWE'S OIL AND GAS LAW IN A NUTSHELL, Second Edition, 465 pages, 1988. Softcover. (Text)

Partnership—see Agency— Partnership

Patent and Copyright Law

MILLER AND DAVIS' INTELLECTUAL PROPERTY—PATENTS, TRADEMARKS AND COPYRIGHT IN A NUTSHELL, Second Edition, 437 pages, 1990. Softcover. (Text)

Products Liability

PHILLIPS' PRODUCTS LIABILITY IN A NUTSHELL, Third Edition, 307 pages, 1988. Softcover. (Text)

Professional Responsibility

ARONSON AND WECKSTEIN'S PROFESSIONAL RESPONSIBILITY IN A NUTSHELL, Second Edition, approximately 500 pages, 1991. Softcover. (Text)

ROTUNDA'S BLACK LETTER ON PROFESSIONAL RESPONSIBILITY, Second Edition, 414 pages, 1988. Softcover. (Review)

WOLFRAM'S HORNBOOK ON

Professional Responsibility— Continued

MODERN LEGAL ETHICS, Student Edition, 1120 pages, 1986. (Text)

Property—see also Real Estate Transactions, Land Use, Trusts and Estates

BERNHARDT'S BLACK LETTER ON PROPERTY, Second Edition, approximately 375 pages, 1991. Softcover. (Review)

BERNHARDT'S REAL PROPERTY IN A NUTSHELL, Second Edition, 448 pages, 1981. Softcover. (Text)

BURKE'S PERSONAL PROPERTY IN A NUTSHELL, 322 pages, 1983. Softcover. (Text)

CUNNINGHAM, STOEBUCK AND WHITMAN'S HORNBOOK ON THE LAW OF PROPERTY, Student Edition, 916 pages, 1984, with 1987 pocket part. (Text)

HILL'S LANDLORD AND TENANT LAW IN A NUTSHELL, Second Edition, 311 pages, 1986. Softcover. (Text)

Real Estate Transactions

BRUCE'S REAL ESTATE FINANCE IN A NUTSHELL, Third Edition, approximately 270 pages, 1991. Softcover. (Text)

NELSON AND WHITMAN'S BLACK LETTER ON LAND TRANSACTIONS AND FINANCE, Second Edition, 466 pages, 1988. Softcover. (Review)

NELSON AND WHITMAN'S HORNBOOK ON REAL ESTATE FINANCE LAW, Second Edition, 941 pages, 1985 with 1989 pocket part. (Text)

Regulated Industries—see also Mass Communication Law, Banking Law

GELLHORN AND PIERCE'S REGULATED INDUSTRIES IN A NUTSHELL, Second Edition, 389 pages, 1987. Softcover. (Text)

Remedies

DOBBS' HORNBOOK ON REMEDIES, 1067 pages, 1973. (Text)

DOBBYN'S INJUNCTIONS IN A NUTSHELL, 264 pages, 1974. Softcover. (Text)

FRIEDMAN'S CONTRACT REMEDIES IN A NUTSHELL, 323 pages, 1981. Softcover. (Text)

O'CONNELL'S REMEDIES IN A NUTSHELL, Second Edition, 320 pages, 1985. Softcover. (Text)

Sea, Law of

SOHN AND GUSTAFSON'S THE LAW OF THE SEA IN A NUTSHELL, 264 pages, 1984. Softcover. (Text)

X

Securities Regulation

HAZEN'S HORNBOOK ON THE LAW OF SECURITIES REGULATION, Second Edition, Student Edition, 1082 pages, 1990. (Text)

RATNER'S SECURITIES REGULATION IN A NUTSHELL, Third Edition, 316 pages, 1988. Softcover. (Text)

SECURITIES REGULATION, SELECTED STATUTES, RULES, AND FORMS. Softcover. 1331 pages, 1991.

Sports Law

SCHUBERT, SMITH AND TRENTADUE'S SPORTS LAW, 395 pages, 1986. (Text)

Tax Practice and Procedure

MORGAN'S TAX PROCEDURE AND TAX FRAUD IN A NUTSHELL, 400 pages, 1990. Softcover. (Text)

Taxation—Corporate

SCHWARZ AND LATHROPE'S BLACK LETTER ON CORPORATE AND PARTNERSHIP TAXATION, Approximately 500 pages, September, 1991 Pub. Softcover. (Review)

WEIDENBRUCH AND BURKE'S FEDERAL INCOME TAXATION OF CORPORATIONS AND STOCKHOLDERS IN A NUTSHELL, Third Edition, 309 pages, 1989. Soft-

cover. (Text)

Taxation—Estate & Gift—see also Estate Planning, Trusts and Estates

MCNULTY'S FEDERAL ESTATE AND GIFT TAXATION IN A NUTSHELL, Fourth Edition, 496 pages, 1989. Softcover. (Text)

Taxation—Individual

HUDSON AND LIND'S BLACK LETTER ON FEDERAL INCOME TAXATION, Third Edition, 406 pages, 1990. Softcover. (Review)

MCNULTY'S FEDERAL INCOME TAXATION OF INDIVIDUALS IN A NUTSHELL, Fourth Edition, 503 pages, 1988. Softcover. (Text)

POSIN'S HORNBOOK ON FEDERAL INCOME TAXATION, Student Edition, 491 pages, 1983, with 1989 pocket part. (Text)

ROSE AND CHOMMIE'S HORNBOOK ON FEDERAL INCOME TAXATION, Third Edition, 923 pages, 1988, with 1989 pocket part. (Text)

Taxation—International

DOERNBERG'S INTERNATIONAL TAXATION IN A NUTSHELL, 325 pages, 1989. Softcover. (Text)

BISHOP AND BROOKS' FEDERAL

Trial and Appellate Advocacy—Continued

(Text)

Trusts and Estates

ATKINSON'S HORNBOOK ON WILLS, Second Edition, 975 pages, 1953. (Text)

AVERILL'S UNIFORM PROBATE CODE IN A NUTSHELL, Second Edition, 454 pages, 1987. Softcover. (Text)

BOGERT'S HORNBOOK ON TRUSTS, Sixth Edition, Student Edition, 794 pages, 1987. (Text)

MCGOVERN, KURTZ AND REIN'S HORNBOOK ON WILLS, TRUSTS AND ESTATES–INCLUDING TAXATION AND FUTURE INTERESTS, 996 pages, 1988. (Text)

MENNELL'S WILLS AND TRUSTS IN A NUTSHELL, 392 pages, 1979. Softcover. (Text)

SIMES' HORNBOOK ON FUTURE

INTERESTS, Second Edition, 355 pages, 1966. (Text)

TURANO AND RADIGAN'S HORNBOOK ON NEW YORK ESTATE ADMINISTRATION, 676 pages, 1986. (Text)

WAGGONER'S FUTURE INTERESTS IN A NUTSHELL, 361 pages, 1981. Softcover. (Text)

Water Law—see also Environmental Law

GETCHES' WATER LAW IN A NUTSHELL, Second Edition, 459 pages, 1990. Softcover. (Text)

Wills—see Trusts and Estates

Workers' Compensation

HOOD, HARDY AND LEWIS' WORKERS' COMPENSATION AND EMPLOYEE PROTECTION LAWS IN A NUTSHELL, Second Edition, 361 pages, 1990. Softcover. (Text)

Advisory Board

JUDICIAL PROCESS
IN A NUTSHELL

SECOND EDITION

By

William L. Reynolds
Professor of Law
University of Maryland School of Law

ST. PAUL, MINN.
WEST PUBLISHING CO.
1991

Nutshell Series, In a Nutshell, the Nutshell Logo and the WP symbol are registered trademarks of West Publishing Co. Registered in the U.S.
Patent and Trademark Office.

COPYRIGHT © 1980 WEST PUBLISHING CO.
COPYRIGHT © 1991 By WEST PUBLISHING CO.
                    50 West Kellogg Boulevard
                    P.O. Box 64526
                    St. Paul, MN 55164–0526

Library of Congress Cataloging-in-Publication Data

Reynolds, William L., 1945–
    Judicial process in a nutshell / by William L. Reynolds. — 2nd
ed.
        p.   cm. — (Nutshell series)
    Includes index.
    ISBN 0–314–88430–0
    1. Judicial process—United States. 2. Law—United States
—Interpretation and construction. I. Title. II. Series.
KF8700.Z9R4   1991
347.73'1—dc20
[347.3071]
                                                    91–17965
                                                        CIP

ISBN 0–314–88430–0

Reynolds, Jud.Proc.2d Ed. NS

To Teddy

*

XVII

FOREWORD TO THE SECOND EDITION

The revisions in the second edition of this *Nutshell* include a new chapter on constitutional interpretation, a topic of great current interest. The unexpected revival of the plain meaning rule in statutory construction, the retreat concerning implied causes of action as well as a number of other changes in the law are also reflected in this edition.

I wish to thank my colleague Dave Bogen, for his helpful comments, my secretary, Kathy Montroy, and my research assistant, Linda M. Thomas, for their indispensable assistance. My wife, Teddy, and my children, Bill, Catherine, and Sarah, all provided immeasurable support. The University of Maryland School of Law has generously supported my work in both editions.

WILLIAM L. REYNOLDS
Baltimore, Maryland

July, 1991

*

XIX

FOREWORD TO THE FIRST EDITION

This *Nutshell* explores the process by which American judges decide cases. Questions involving both common law adjudication and statutory interpretation are analyzed. Constitutional decision-making and problems concerning the trial of issues are touched upon but lightly; each of those areas requires a book of its own. Although the book has been written with the law student primarily in mind, I hope and believe that it will be of interest and use to others who are interested in the process we use in passing judgment on claims of right.

The author of a book such as this has many persons to thank. My own interest in the subject of this *Nutshell* began in law school in the course in Legal Process. Then Professor (and now Dean) Albert Sacks stimulated us in the classroom and the wonderful materials of that name, prepared by him and the late Professor Henry Hart (discussed further in § 4.2), forced the students to open the windows of their minds. It was altogether a rare intellectual experience, one whose imprint can be found throughout this *Nutshell*. Later, at Maryland, I had the opportunity to teach a course in

Legal Process, where my students and I studied the subject together.

Judge Frank A. Kaufman of the United States District Court for the District of Maryland, for whom I clerked, helped show me how a wise jurist, interested in both justice and law, practices his craft. I have been fortunate in having worked on articles in collaboration with two authors who have provided me with much guidance in the quest for understanding of these issues: John F. Davis, now a Visiting Professor at Maryland, formerly Assistant Solicitor General and Clerk of the Supreme Court; and Professor William Richman of the University of Toledo School of Law, former student and present friend.

The support provided by the administration and my colleagues at Maryland has been outstanding. Kenneth Abraham, Dave Bogen, John Ester, Everett Goldberg, Bill Hall, Alan Hornstein, Bill Richman, Ted Tomlinson, Joel Woodey, and Greg Young read drafts of portions of the book. Their comments were invaluable; the standard disclaimer is in order. Kathleen Morris and Deborah Robinson, both students at Maryland, have provided splendid research and editorial assistance.

Indispensable to the completion of this book was the patient and intelligent assistance provided by the faculty secretaries at Maryland. All have contributed to the finished product, but Gail Batts deserves special mention for her help in making a complex and difficult task, manageable. My thanks to all.

Finally, the support given me in this project by my wife, Teddy, and our children, Bill, Catherine, and Sarah, provided comfort and encouragement beyond measure.

WLR

Baltimore, Maryland
April, 1980

*

OUTLINE

Part C. More on Understanding

Part D. Subsequent Developments

*

TABLE OF CASES

References are to Pages

A

B

E

F.

G

H

I

J

N

O

P

R

S

T

U

V

W

*

JUDICIAL PROCESS
IN A NUTSHELL
SECOND EDITION

*

CHAPTER ONE
INTRODUCTION

§ 1.1 A Prefatory Note

This is a book about how judges in American courts decide cases, that is, problems brought before them for resolution. The approach to that process reflects a court's view of its role in society.

Attitudes toward that role have varied greatly during our history. At times judges have viewed their role as passive and have been reluctant to interfere with the traditions of the past. At other times courts have been avowedly innovative, believing it their duty to shape the law in order better to advance their own vision of society. More often, of course, judges work between those opposing views.

American judges fully recognize, whatever their view of their function, that their decisions make law. In deciding what course to follow many considerations come into play. Judges may decide that a particular rule is desirable because it furthers economic goals (such as the protection of contracts), or social goals (protecting us from invasions of our privacy), or moral goals (not permitting the punishment of insane persons), or institutional goals (reducing judicial workload). A judge's decisions, therefore, are normative as well as political. But it would be a mistake to believe that the typical judge thinks of herself as a philosopher or political scientist. Rather, she views her job as a lawyer's task, the application of legal principles by the judicial process to a set of facts.

Commentators on our legal system, like the judges themselves, have also advanced various views of the proper role of a judge. This diversity should not be surprising because the nature of those views relates closely to the concept of how the judicial process should operate, and there have been many different views on that subject.

Nevertheless, it is possible to speak with some assurance about the subjects covered in this book. In the first place, there *is* a good deal of consensus, in this country at least, on many of these issues. Where that consensus is lacking, the main lines of analysis can be delineated and my own solution of the problem offered (exposing in the process my own jurisprudential leanings). Finally, whatever answers are given, it is important that students (and lawyers and judges, too) think about how cases are decided and law declared. Consideration of those topics is essential to an understanding of our legal system.

§ 1.2 Bibliography

The problems of the judicial process, unlike those of many other areas of the law, do not generally lend themselves to definitive resolution by case or statute. Much of the discussion and authority comes from secondary sources such as articles and books. Consequently, it seemed wise to include in the text fairly frequent reference to readings which give a good overview of an area under discussion. I hope that the reader will be stimulated to pursue some of the matters further.

Commentary on the subjects found in this *Nutshell* can be found in caselaw, casebooks, treatises, and law reviews. Three excellent collections of readings on topics generally covered in this *Nutshell* are Berch and Berch, Introduction to Legal Process and Method (1985); Kelso and Kelso, Studying Law: An Introduction (1984); and Leflar, Appellate Judicial Opinions (1974). The best general commentary can be found in a magnificent book by Karl Llewellyn, The Common Law Tradition: Deciding Appeals (1960), and the best casebook-treatise approach is by Professor Henry Hart and Dean Albert Sacks, The Legal Process: Basic Problems in the Making and Application of Law (tent. ed. 1958); both of these books are discussed in more detail in § 4.2. Two classic works that should be read by all students of this area were written by judges who later became Justices: Benjamin Cardozo, The Nature of the Judicial Process (1921), and Oliver Wendell Holmes, The Path of the Law, 10 Harv.L.Rev. 457 (1897).

CHAPTER TWO
SOURCES OF JUDICIAL POWER

The role a court plays depends upon its position in the structure of government, and upon the power that history and practice have vested in the court. The judicial role should be considered from two perspectives: the *horizontal* position of the judiciary with respect to the other branches of government; and the *vertical* relationship of the several courts in each judicial system.

§ 2.1 Horizontal Power

The governments of the several states and that of the United States are organized on the principle of separation of powers. The judiciary is one of the three branches; hence the courts, collectively, of a jurisdiction are said to be "co-equal" with the executive and the legislative body. That position gives the judiciary, acting within its proper sphere, the power to act as a separate branch of government. Generally in American practice this has meant two different types of power.

a. Supreme Power

In some areas of decision-making the judiciary has asserted virtually uncheckable power. "[I]t is

4

the responsibility of this court to act as the ultimate interpreter of the Constitution," Chief Justice Warren wrote in Powell v. McCormack (1969), and while this assertion is limited to some extent (by notions of justiciability, mootness, and standing, for example, as well as by the amendment process), it is a widely accepted principle of constitutional theory.

A less well known assertion of supreme authority by courts has been in areas held to be inherently within their province. One court noted, for example, that "any legislation undertaking to require judicial action within fixed periods of time is an unconstitutional interference by the legislature with a judicial function." Lindauer v. Allen (1969). Such cases are really constitutional in nature for they are premised on the theory that another branch of government has trespassed on the court's domain, and that the trespass weakens unduly the ability of the court to perform its constitutional functions. Thus, it has been held that a court may compel a city to appropriate funds needed to operate the city's courts. Carroll v. Tate (1971). Cases such as *Lindauer* and *Carroll* demonstrate the resistance of courts to legislative encroachment upon inherent judicial power.

b. *Limited Power*

The vast majority of judicial work, however, lies in the area where the other branches of government share power with the court. Contract, tort, and property law, for example, lie within the proper domain of both court and legislature, for in those areas each branch can make law to control the disposition of disputes. Because those disputes do not generally involve constitutional issues, or ones inherently judicial in nature, the legislature has the final say as to the content of the law. In this area between legislature and court, therefore, the former is supreme; a statute, in other words, can change the law already established by a court. Thus, the power of the judiciary in contracts can be, and has been, limited by exercises of legislative power.

§ 2.2 Vertical Power

Judicial systems are hierarchic. Typically, in American jurisdictions there is an inferior trial court (or perhaps more than one), a trial court of general jurisdiction, an intermediate appellate court, and, finally, an appellate court of last resort. (There is also often a group of specialized courts to handle matters such as tax and probate.) A firm line of authority prevails within this system, for each inferior court is expected to obey the commands of those courts superior to it.

Superiority, however, does not cut across jurisdictional lines. An inferior Maryland state court has no obligation to follow a decision of the California Supreme Court, or even to follow a decision of the Supreme Court of the United States—unless the decision of the latter is on a constitutional question or an interpretation of applicable federal law. In that event, the decision of the Supreme Court must be followed by the Maryland court dealing with a problem of federal law, for the Maryland court then is, in effect, operating within the federal system.

Because lines of formal authority run only within a system, it is necessary to know in which system a particular problem occurs.

§ 2.3   The Common Law—A Very Brief History

The express assertion of power by the judiciary to declare law, an assertion in which the executive and legislature readily acquiesce, may seem surprising in a nation where democratic principles are rooted as deeply as ours. There is, after all, little that is democratic about the judicial system. Judges, especially appellate judges, are not always elected; even where they must submit themselves to voter approval there often is little or no contest. Hence, the electorate rarely exercises direct control over the judiciary. Why then is there general acceptance of this power to make law? At least a large part of the answer can be found in history.

English kings in the medieval period established a system of central courts to administer justice throughout the land. The law that they administered—common to the entire realm (unlike the law associated with specialized courts such as admiralty)—became known as "common law." By the time Sir William Blackstone wrote his great Commentaries on the Common Law (1765–69), common law was associated with unwritten law (*lex non scripta*), that is, law derived not from a legislative source (*lex scripta*), but from the "general custom" of the English people. The common law judges themselves were seen by Blackstone as the "living oracles of the law," Commentaries 69, and through them the habits of a people spoke with the force of law. Judges spoke through the cases they decided, decisions that served as guides or precedents for future decisions.

The King's justice was administered by these courts through a series of writs designed to provide remedies for various problems. Inevitably, the writs shaped the growth of substantive law; but, at least in its early stages, the law was creative. The writ of trespass, for example, evolved into the bodies of law that we know today as tort and contract. As might be expected, the system, although creative at times, became more rigid as it matured. One way of circumventing the rigidity was through legal fictions such as the jurisdictional allegation that a defendant lived in "the parish of St. Mary le Bow, in the ward of Cheap", an allegation that was non-traversable (not subject to challenge), no matter where the defendant in fact lived. The effect of such fictions was to maintain formally the rules of the past while eliminating much of their inconvenience. The common law never lost completely its capacity for creative growth, however.

The common law courts were not the only source of judicial authority in England, however, and other courts competed with them for judicial business. Among these were the admiralty and ecclesiastical courts (described so beautifully by Dickens in *David Copperfield*) and, most prominent, the court of equity under the head of the Chancellor. Each of these courts left a mark on our jurisprudence, but it is the influence of equity that is felt most keenly today. Equity was the judicial arm of the Chancellor, a royal executive officer; the court of equity was separate from the common law courts. The Chancellor sitting in equity tried to perform justice on a more individualized basis than the King's courts. It was said that matters were referred to the "conscience" of the Chancellor. Because it was more flexible than the common law, and acted more rapidly, equity became a sought after alternative to common law courts. Not surprisingly, the two clashed—a drama played out against the larger stage of the fight to limit the power of the Stuart Kings. Eventually, accommodation was reached, a story best left for others. (Equity also became as rigid and inflexible as the common law ever was, as Dickens described in *Bleak House*.) But the influence of equity survives in this country. A few states, for example, have separate "law" and "equity" courts, each with its own rules of procedure. "Equitable" remedies are said not to be available unless "legal" remedies are inadequate; specific performance of a construction contract, for example, will not be ordered if damages prove to be a sufficient remedy. On the other side, there is the tradition of equitable relief, of the Chancellor acting swiftly and with dispatch to "do justice." Symbolic here is the example of school desegregation, accomplished largely by judges using creatively the tools of equity.

Settlement of the American colonies brought with it the English legal system. Although some of the transplants were bizarre, survivors of medieval times in a frontier society, American adaptation of English law adjusted quickly and well to the needs of a society far different economically and socially from England. As American society became more settled, the judicial systems of the colonies grew to resemble more closely that of the mother country. Complete congruence was prevented, however, by different circumstances and the scarcity of American lawyers and judges rigorously trained in the subtleties of the common law.

With independence the new states did not reject their heritage of English law. Instead, the states provided for "reception" of the common law. Typical is the provision in the Maryland Declaration of Rights of 1776, guaranteeing "the Common Law of England and the trial by Jury" along with such English statutes adopted prior to June 1, 1774, "which, by experience, have been found applicable to * * * local and other circumstances * * *." As the new nation expanded west the common law, and the tradition of judge-made law, went with it. Along the way it conquered or, at times, compromised with Spanish and French law. In the two centuries of our independence American common law decision-making has survived numerous attacks. These have ranged from Anglophobia in the early days of the Republic to broadbased movements to "codify" (enact by legislation) the law. Despite such movements, law making by judges—what we call "common law"—is alive and well today. This is surely due to a number of factors, among them inertia and the reluctance of the bench to surrender a hard-won skill. Most important, perhaps, is a belief that common law decision-making works—that it provides a very acceptable addition to legislative and executive action. (See also Part C of Chapter IV.)

A note on terminology is necessary here. Although the term "common law" has, as noted earlier in this section, a strict definition, the phrase is also used extensively in this country to refer to law generally made by judges (*lex non scripta*) as opposed to that made by the legislature (*lex scripta*). It will be so used in this *Nutshell*.

CHAPTER THREE
CRAFTSMANSHIP

Craftsmanship—the manner in which the court goes about its decision-making process—matters. Sloppy procedures and sloppy methods of making decisions lead to sloppy decisions. This is not just a matter of aesthetics (although that should also be important); good decision-making techniques are essential to achieve proper decisions. Yet craftsmanship is too often overlooked; most lawyers and judges would agree with Justice Brandeis' observation that, "it is more important that the applicable rule be settled than that it be settled right." Burnet v. Coronado Oil & Gas Co. (1932). Although it is understandable that questions of substance take precedence over those of craftsmanship, attention must be paid the latter if a court is to perform efficiently and do justice.

§ 3.1 The Opinion

Judicial decisions often are rendered in the form of an opinion, a statement by a judge explaining why she decided the case the way she did. In some jurisdictions this practice is a constitutional requirement. Opinion writing is by no means universal, however, and, even when it is mandatory, there are often significant gaps in the court's opinion. Nevertheless, in trial courts in which sufficient time is available, and in appellate courts, a decision is more likely to be in opinion form. As the opinion has evolved in America the legal community has come to expect that the opinion will contain a summary of the case, a statement of facts, an explanation of the road to the result, and a record of the decision.

Courts that consist of several judges have used a number of methods in delivering opinions. In some courts it has been traditional to speak with a unified voice; indeed, until fairly recently, European courts generally delivered an opinion which gave no hint of either authorship or the existence of division among the judges. Common law courts, however, have generally made known both authorship and the presence of disagreement. They believe that doing so encourages judicial responsibility, for anonymity is not available to shield the writer of an inferior opinion, and the availability of dissent permits a reader of the opinion to infer from the absence of dissent that other members of the court agree with the position taken by the opinion.

Some courts have taken the position that each judge should deliver an individual opinion in every case. The practice in the very early Supreme Court, for example, was to render opinions *seriatim*. Since the days of John Marshall, however, American courts have generally thought it proper to speak whenever possible through an opinion identified as the voice of the court, although an occasional lament for the old practice can be found. E.g., Graves v. New York ex rel. O'Keefe (1939) (Frankfurter, J., concurring). The opinion of the court carries with it in most cases the name of an author, and is joined by as many members of the court as wish to be associated with it.

There are several advantages to the unified opinion. The first is judicial *economy,* for the preparation of an opinion (especially if it is to be published) consumes a great deal of time and energy. A reduction in the number of opinions issued should, therefore, reduce the *time* spent on them. Second, an "opinion of the court" carries *authority,* speaking as it does as the voice of a branch of government. Brown v. Board of Educ. (1954), the *School Desegregation Case,* illustrates this vividly. In talking of that case, Chief Justice Warren remembered the long and hard effort by the Supreme Court to reach agreement on an opinion that would be unanimous, thus permitting the Justices to present to the nation the picture of a Court united behind its pronouncement that segregated education is inherently unequal. A final advantage of the unified opinion is *certainty.* An opinion clearly addressed to a problem states the solution the court sees; a reader interested in that solution can find it and understand it with less effort and less possibility of confusion than if it were necessary to compare several slightly different opinions.

The advantages of a unified opinion of a court also suggest its disadvantages. In the first place, we may not want to save judicial time in this fashion, for if each judge must express his ideas on the case in writing, he may well find his ideas changed in the process. Even if not, the self-education so provided may lead to a better understanding of the situation and application of the court's solution to later problems. In other words, the degree of concentration a judge applies to a problem is linked with the quality of justice—present and future—that the judge dispenses. Although this position is a valid one, very few American appellate courts today have the luxury to engage in it.

A different objection to the unified opinion has been advanced by a distinguished judge, Schaefer, Precedent and Policy, 34 U.Chi.L.Rev. 3 (1966). Justice Schaefer suggested that *more* certainty will be achieved by opinions *seriatim,* on the theory that if each judge's view on a problem is known it will be possible for the court's audience to predict the future decisions of each with more assurance. There are, however, several problems with that position. First, as Justice Schaefer observed, it is doubtful whether many counsel and judges have the time—and perhaps the ability—to analyze multiple opinions with the necessary care to make the effort worthwhile. A second counter to his argument stems from the probability that the common "holding" derived from this type of approach will be relatively narrow, leading to diminution of broad principles in the case law, an absence which will, in turn, slow down the development of the law.

§ 3.2 Some Mechanics of Opinion Formulation

Traditionally, in the Supreme Court, the Chief Justice, following a conference and tentative vote on the case, assigns the drafting of the Court's opinion to himself or to some other member of the preliminary majority. If the Chief Justice is not part of that majority, the assignment is made by the senior Associate Justice among the tentative majority. The assignment power is most important, for it can be used to reward or punish Justices, or to try to expand or restrict the scope of the decision.

The draft opinion (along with any dissents) circulates among the Court and members may make suggestions for change, sometimes linking continued adherence to the opinion to acceptance of the suggested changes. The bargaining may be over fundamental changes in the draft of the opinion or it may be over matters that are relatively minor in the present case but which may be of significance in the future. Obviously, bargaining among the Justices can and does go on, and the opinion issued as that "of the Court", may not reflect precisely the writer's own views. The compromise process is important, for it may lead to a more convoluted, less coherent opinion for the Court than otherwise would have been the case.

Most courts of last resort probably act in similar fashion. As time pressures grow more intense, departure from that model will probably be stronger. Some judges of intermediate appellate courts have commented on the deference given the author of an opinion—a deference arising from lack of time of other judges to review the product. The difficulties with the model become even more acute with recognition that on some courts central staff clerks prepare draft opinions, drafts which may end up (with little or no change) as the "opinion of the court."

Sometimes an opinion will not carry an author's name but simply be identified as *"Per Curiam."* Generally, this type of disposition is reserved for cases deemed routine, squarely controlled by precedent. Sometimes, however, a *per curiam* is apparently used to permit the court to control the disposition of a case without writing an opinion explaining that result. Following Brown v. Board of Educ. (1954), the Court disposed of challenges to segregation of public facilities in contexts other than education in a series of *per curiam* decisions. E.g., Holmes v. City of Atlanta (1955) (municipal golf courses). It was certainly not clear from *Brown* that all public segregation was, as a general principle, unconstitutional. For the Court to have issued a full opinion in each of those cases, however, would have required an explication of *Brown* that perhaps the Court was not able or willing to provide. Rather than discard unanimity, the Court disposed of those cases summarily. But the *per curiam* decisions were not without effect. In the end the Court was able to say with respect to segregated courtrooms, "It is no longer open to question that a State may not constitutionally require segregation of public facilities," Johnson v. Virginia (1963). The series of *per curiam* decisions thus had ultimately extended *Brown* without explicating the basis for that extension.

§ 3.3 Separate Opinions

Unanimous decisions are the desired norm in most American appellate courts. On occasion, however, a judge will feel that he should issue an opinion separate from that of "the court." If his opinion would lead to a disposition of the case different from that reached by the majority it is a dissent; otherwise, it is a concurrence.

Separate opinions have long been thought proper in most common law courts. That belief perhaps reflects the tradition of opinions delivered *seriatim*. The growth of the unified opinion carried with it a reduction in the frequency of separate opinions; they were rare, for example, on the Marshall Court of the early Nineteenth Century. As the Supreme Court after the Civil War became embroiled in constitutional matters separate opinions became more common. As late as 1905, however, Justice Holmes felt obliged to begin his great dissent in

Lochner v. New York (1905), with an apology: "I regret sincerely that I am unable to agree with the judgment in this case, and that I think it my duty to express my dissent." Since then, however, dissents and concurrences on the Supreme Court have become so common that judicial disagreement has long been a subject of critical concern. Their continued widespread use suggests that the functions served by separate opinions are important—at least to the judges.

Although dissents and concurrences are similar in many respects they serve somewhat different ends. They will therefore be explored separately.

§ 3.4   The Dissent

Dissents serve a myriad of useful purposes. They restrain the judicial advocate, they encourage judicial responsibility, and they appeal to outside audiences for correction of perceived mistakes of the majority. The last is perhaps the most widely appreciated reason for dissent; Justice Holmes, for example, earned his sobriquet, "The Great Dissenter," on the basis of his dissents which later became law. Chief Justice Hughes wrote that a dissent is "an appeal to the brooding spirit of the law, to the intelligence of a later day." C. Hughes, The Supreme Court of the United States 68 (1928). In this form the dissent is a judge's cry of anguish, an appeal for later vindication. The appeal may be general or it may be addressed to a more discrete audience: perhaps to a higher court to overturn the decision, or to the legislature to accomplish what the dissenter could not.

The dissent could also have been addressed to the other members of the court. A dissent generally circulates well before the majority opinion is issued in the hope that it will convince some other judges to change their vote to a dissent. That apparently is not a rare happening. Even if the dissent does not change enough votes to become a majority opinion, it may restrain the tendency of the majority to become what Holmes called the "judicial advocate." Awareness that one's work may be criticized incisively in public tends to have a marvelous restraining effect. The value of the dissent here is conservative, for it helps prevent a court from embracing new doctrine too quickly and with too little consideration. The mere possibility of a dissent may serve to keep the majority from becoming too adventurous. In short, the dissent can act as a powerful stimulus to judicial restraint and reponsibility.

That argument works in reverse as well. Because dissents are commonplace it seems fair to associate a judge joining an opinion with at least the general content of the opinion. While this may not in fact, as Justice Schaefer has argued, supra § 3.2, be necessarily a fair association, it is one commonly made. A judge, therefore, must think twice before joining in an opinion, even if that agreement is evinced only by a failure to dissent.

Another advantage of the dissent can come about when the dissenter "explains" the majority opinion. That is especially useful when the majority opinion is obscure. Also helpful is the dissenter's addition (or subtraction) from the majority's statement of fact. Not only can a dissenter help the reader understand the majority's opinion, but the dissent also helps keep the majority honest.

Finally, dissents provide a safetyvalve for judicial ire. Blowing off steam in public may be better for judicial harmony than a continual repression of frustration and anger.

Although dissents serve useful purposes they must also be handled with care. A major drawback to their use is that they dispel the myth of judicial harmony. While Justice Douglas was surely right when he said in response to this argument that "confidence based on understanding is more enduring than confidence based on awe," Douglas, The Dissent: A Safeguard of Democracy, 32 J.Am.Jud.Soc. 104 (1948), needless dissent can imperil confidence that the courts are working properly. More important, the dissent, if used too often, may lose its special value as a signal to the bar and public that *this* is a problem of significance. Like the little boy who cried "wolf" too often, the indiscriminate dissenter may find that he has lost his audience. A final problem with dissents inheres in the ability of the dissenter to focus on very specific issues, without need to deal with the problem as a whole. Sometimes the focus on single issues is accompanied by some exaggeration, a tactic dissents find easier to employ successfully.

§ 3.5 The Concurrence

A concurring opinion does not in general differ analytically from a dissent. Agreement with the court's disposition of the problem would seem to be a fortuity, in terms of the writer's attempt to express his displeasure with the majority. A concurrence can also be used to explain a change of heart, or to make a personal statement on the problem at issue. On occasion, however, a concurring opinion apparently is an attempt by the writer to limit the scope of the majority opinion and to explore problems that it presents. Justice Powell, concurring in Runyon v. McCrary (1976), for example, stated his belief that the prohibition of racial discrimination in private schools, accomplished by *Runyon,* would not be extended to very "personal" contracts such as the hiring of a baby-sitter. Justice Powell's expression on that issue is crucial because the issue he addressed is an important one raised by the *Runyon* holding. Because of his position with the majority it is likely that his view will carry more weight than that of a single Justice speaking in isolation.

A concurring opinion in a close case may also be a signal to litigants that there is a weak spot in the majority's armor and that the attack should continue to be pressed. In National League of Cities

v. Usery (1976), for example, Justice Blackmun wrote, "It seems to me that it [the majority opinion] adopts a balancing approach * * *. With this understanding on my part of the Court's opinion, I join it." Although there is little evidence in the majority opinion that it agreed with a "balancing approach," Justice Blackmun's views were important for his was the deciding vote in a 5–4 decision. Nine years later, in Garcia v. San Antonio Metro. Transit Auth. (1985), Justice Blackmun switched sides; this time he wrote the majority opinion which overruled *National League of Cities*.

Sometimes a judge will concur or dissent without explaining his unwillingness to join the majority opinion. Failure to do so is understandable for a judge hard-pressed for adequate time to do his job properly. Yet the court's obligation to decide cases properly before it would seem to extend as well to all those who sit in judgment on the case. A judge owes an explanation to litigants and public alike of his views on the problems presented for decision. Thus, unless the reasons for disagreement are clear from a judge's past pronouncements, reliance on notation of disagreement without an accompanying explanation should be minimized.

A variation on the "notation" approach can be seen in statements which state agreement "dubitante" with the majority opinion. An extreme example of this form is Justice Jackson's statement in United States v. Kahriger (1953), where the Court upheld a federal gambling tax; Jackson "concur[red], but with such doubt that if the minority agreed upon an opinion which did not impair legitimate use of the taxing power I would join it." Such an expression of uncertainty may be appropriate where doubt as to the proper course to follow is strong and the judge's vote will not affect the outcome. And yet perhaps *Kahriger* would have been decided differently if Justice Jackson had attempted to work out in an opinion his problem concerning the "legitimate use" of the taxing power. Even if the result remained unchanged, later courts would have had the benefit of Jackson's proposed solution—or, at least, his thoughts on why possible solutions to the problem would not work.

§ 3.6 Plurality Opinions

Failure of any opinion to command the adherence of a majority of the court results in decisions by plurality. Sometimes it is hard to discern whether an opinion represents a majority, especially if one member of the putative majority writes a concurring opinion with a point of view markedly different from that of the "majority." The Supreme Court has solved this problem by label: If a Justice speaks only for a plurality, the first opinion begins with the phrase, "Justice A announced the judgment of the Court and an opinion in which Justice B and Justice C join."

Plurality decisions represent a form of decision by *seriatim* opinion discussed earlier. Like concurring and dissenting opinions, plurality decisions are rare in most state courts; in recent years, however, they have appeared fairly frequently in the Supreme Court. Some of the plurality decisions have been downright bizarre. Two examples illustrate their paradoxical character. In National Mutual Ins. Co. v. Tidewater Transfer Co., Inc. (1949), the question before the Court was whether Congress had constitutional authority to grant citizens of the District of Columbia access to federal courts. Three Justices thought Congress had power to do so under Article I of the United States Constitution, but *not* under Article III; three others believed that there was such power in Congress under Article III, but *not* under Article I; the remaining two participating Justices believed Congress completely lacked power so to legislate. In sum, while an absolute majority of the Court believed Congress lacked power under *either* Article to do what it had done, the statute was upheld.

Even stranger is Oregon v. Mitchell (1970), a challenge to the extension by Congress of the right to vote in state and federal elections to eighteen-year olds. Eight members of the Court thought that whatever power Congress had, it was the same for state and federal elections. Four of the eight thought Congress had full power to extend the vote, the other four believed Congress lacked that power. The ninth member of the Court, Justice Black, was the only one who believed Congress had authority to extend the vote only in federal elections. Because of the make-up of the Court on the issues, Justice Black's view became the law of the land, even though it had been expressly repudiated by eight Justices.

Decisions like those do little to foster public confidence in the Court's performance. Even the more routine plurality decisions, moreover, can lead to confusion both within the Court itself and among those who must interpret its decisions. Those problems stem from the fact that a court does not speak with an institutional voice when it makes a plurality decision. Thus, none of the opinions in a plurality decision is of binding precedential value. Miller v. California (1973).

There are, however, partial palliatives available and sometimes used by the Court. One involves the use of a short *per curiam* by the Court to accompany the decision and explain its understanding of what it has done. This technique has not been used often, and seems to be reserved for only the most important of cases. It has been used, for example, in Regents of the Univ. of Calif. v. Bakke (1978), and New York Times Co. v. United States (1971), to reduce the confusion created by the multiplicity of opinions in those cases. A second technique that lessens the uncertainty of a plurality decision requires the consumer of the decision to ascertain if there is common ground among the several opinions, ground shared by a majority of the Court. One of the Supreme Court's obscenity decisions illustrates this well. In the *Fanny Hill* case, A Book Named "John Cleland's

Memoirs of a Woman of Pleasure" v. Attorney
General (1966), three members of the Court
thought the proper standard to test for obscenity
was whether the work was utterly without redeeming social value; two other Justices believed no
standard could survive constitutional challenge;
and one of the Justices argued that "hard-core"
pornography could be suppressed, but failed to
define the term. It could be said, therefore, after
Fanny Hill, that in order to find a book obscene,
the book must, *at the least,* be "utterly without
redeeming social value."

In Regents of the Univ. of California v. Bakke
(1978), the Supreme Court used a third method for
minimizing the confusion created by a plurality
decision. Plaintiff in *Bakke* challenged a medical
school's affirmative action program. The Supreme
Court, in shifting majorities, ruled that while the
program in question was illegal, not all affirmative
action programs were. The swing vote on these
issues was Justice Powell, whose opinion had no
other adherents. In a highly unusual move, Powell's opinion was made the lead opinion for the
Court. The emphasis placed on the opinion of a
single Justice by the Court suggests that the Court
was signaling its audience that a plan which followed Justice Powell's approach would be valid.
That signal—widely interpreted as such in initial
reactions to the *Bakke* decision—helped to keep to
a minimum the disruption of the nation's many
affirmative action programs.

§ 3.7 Separate Opinions in State Appellate Courts

Concern over too many dissents generally extends only to the work of the Supreme Court, for the state courts of last resort have not in general been nearly as divisive. In its October, 1989 Term, for example, the Supreme Court achieved unanimity in less than a quarter of its decisions. Data on state courts are hard to come by but suggest that disagreement in more than a quarter of the decisions would be unusual.

That difference is not surprising. State courts generally receive far less critical attention than the Supreme Court, lessening a judge's need constantly to explain his own opinion to critics. Thus, the existence of an audience may generate work designed to reach that audience. Similarly, the cases presented to state courts probably contain fewer volatile issues than do those that reach the Supreme Court. State courts typically hear more cases dealing with relatively well-settled matters than the Supreme Court, and the issues heard tend to be less emotional—fewer significant constitutional matters are heard by state courts, for example. The more volatile an issue the more likely that a judge will be provoked to "appeal to the bar of history" through a separate opinion. In such cases, what Justice Schaefer has termed the "fighting conviction" of the dissenter necessary to break ranks is most likely to be stirred.

§ 3.8   The Equally Divided Court

On rare occasions, a court will divide equally on the disposition of the case. The effect of that division is to affirm the decision below. The affirmance follows from the belief that the decision below stands until a majority of a higher court decides otherwise. Because there is no decision as such, affirmance by an equally divided court lacks precedential value. United States v. Pink (1942).

A specialized problem in this area involves an appellate court's *en banc* review of a decision of one of its panels. Does the equal split of the full court affirm the panel's decision or that of the court below? The United States Courts of Appeals have ruled that the opinion of the District Court should be affirmed in that situation, apparently on the theory that the panel decision is "vacated" or withdrawn by the order taking the case for *en banc* review. See, e.g., Bernstein v. Nationwide Mutual Ins. Co. (1972). That seems correct for if the panel decision were to stand it would have precedential value (at least if published; see § 3.9). The panel's decision would thus be a precedent of the Court of Appeals even though the *full* Court of Appeals had declined to adopt it as a precedent. Hence, the only decision that can stand as a precedent is the decision below.

When the Supreme Court affirms by an equally divided court no announcement is made of which members were on each side or of any of the thinking of the individual Justices. Other courts, however, sometimes provide both a scoreboard and explanation even though the court has neither decided anything nor—as a result—established precedent. Thus, such expressions are *dicta*. (See infra, § 4.14). One judge has suggested that the scoreboard and explanations are designed to suggest to the Supreme Court that "because we are divided it should take jurisdiction." Carter v. United States (1963) (Jones, J., concurring specially). The explanations can also be confusing, for a less than careful reader may believe the lead opinion is the opinion of the court.

§ 3.9 Publication of Opinions

For many hundreds of years knowledge of the common law depended upon unofficial reports of cases, reports made by persons charged with no official duty to do so. The famous Year Books, for example, which go back to the Thirteenth Century and the time of Edward I, started as notes kept by students. Later, prestigious jurists such as Coke and Blackstone published edited versions of cases they had judged or of which they had knowledge. Such reporting was necessarily selective, and many cases never saw print, vanishing forever. It has only been in the last hundred years that English cases have been systematically reported under official auspices. See Veeder, The English Reports, 1292–1865, 15 Harv.L.Rev. 1 and 109 (1901).

American reports also began informally. Reports of colonial cases apparently circulated only in manuscript, and publication did not begin until after the American Revolution. Quickly, however, American entrepreneurs began printing case reports, and it was not long before states began issuing official reports of cases. Near the end of the Nineteenth Century the West Publishing Company began the National Reporter System, collecting cases in a series of six Regional Reporters (a system so efficient that in recent years a number of states have stopped issuing official reports). Today an array of specialized reporters is also available, covering fields from admiralty to zoning; a curious feature of these reporters is that they sometimes report cases which a judge has not sent out for general publication. Computer databases also contain many opinions—both published and unpublished.

Not all opinions are published; after all, not all opinions are even written. Courts of last resort generally publish most of their decisions, while publication is less frequent in intermediate appellate courts, and unusual among trial courts.

The last two or three decades have seen a retreat from the belief that most decisions of appellate courts should be published. Perceiving possibilities of saving judicial time in the preparation of opinions for publication, along with savings for consumers of opinions (less research, fewer books to store), a number of courts have limited publication of their opinions. Limitation generally occurs when an opinion does not make, change, or criticize law; in other words an opinion will only be published if the court believes it should be generally available as a precedent. See Reynolds & Richman, The Non–Precedential Precedent—Limited Publication and No Citation Rules in the United States Court of Appeals, 78 Col.L.Rev. 1167 (1978). As a result, today, fewer than half of the decisions of the United States Courts of Appeals are published.

Along with limited publication, the courts have imposed rules limiting the effect of the unpublished decision; typically, it will have no precedential effect (other than res judicata, collateral estoppel, and law of the case), nor can it be cited as a precedent. Those requirements are imposed to insure that the limited publication schemes are not wrecked by "covert" publication and research. The effect is to make unpublished opinions non-law since they have no effect beyond the case at bar. This has been thought permissible because the courts have limited use of the non-publication option to routine cases and those involving issues where ample precedent is available. In such cases, it is felt, there is no need for a circle wider than the litigants to be aware of the case and its disposition.

Limited publication plans respond to a real need created by the pressure we place on courts. They have, however, unfortunate side effects. In the first place, the rules are difficult for the judges to follow; commentators have found numerous examples of unpublished decisions which *do* break new ground or which are inconsistent with other decisions of the same court. Because this happens, sophisticated litigants often review unpublished decisions, lessening the potential of unpublished opinions for reducing the cost of doing legal research.

More important, limited publication diminishes both judicial responsibility and accountability. The threat to judicial responsibility can take several forms. A decision insulated from the operation of precedent is one that a judge might be less careful in thinking about and writing; after all, the opinion will have no real effect beyond the litigants. Worse, if she has decided that the opinion is routine (and not to be published), she may not devote enough attention to the case to see if in fact her original diagnosis of routine was correct. Less than full care in decision-making may also feed on itself, leading to a habit of sloppy decisions. Finally, the unpublished list is a convenient place for a court to unload opinions in areas where it is unwilling (or unable) to make its decisions known; that is, limited publication can be used deliberately by a court to avoid deciding according to the rules of *stare decisis*.

Limited publication also threatens judicial accountability. The opinion may be too truncated for effective review by a higher court. Limited publication also hampers review by other members of the court's audience, for the general inaccessibility of unpublished opinions, a necessary commodity for anyone interested in the work of a court, makes it less likely that scholars will be able to work with complete information.

§ 3.10 The Role of the Appellate Court

An appellate court reviews what has happened at a lower level in the judicial hierarchy. An appellate court has the dual function of checking for error below and developing and applying the law in an even-handed way throughout the system. Judge Shirley Hufstedler called those roles of the appellate court, respectively, "the review of correctness" and the "institutional function." Hufstedler, New Blocks for Old Pyramids: Reshaping the Judicial System, 44 S.Cal.L.Rev. 901, 910 (1971). Thus, the appellate court serves both to insure that the decision below was as free of error as possible, and to guide and develop the body of law within the judicial system. The same thought can be captured by labelling the two roles "public" and "private." The public role of the court is to develop law through the creation of precedents. The private role attempts to insure the correctness of the decision.

Many systems have more than one appellate court. In those systems the role of the intermediate court differs from that of the court of last resort. To quote Judge Hufstedler again: "With each rise in the appellate structure the importance of the review for correctness diminishes and the importance of the institutional function increases." That shift is easily explained: With cases coming in from throughout the system, the demands on the time of the highest court dictate that it spend its limited energies on those cases with the widest potential impact. Further, each case that reaches a high court has usually been through one appeal, and there is little reason to believe that a second "review for correctness" will add more than marginally to the likelihood that the decision in the case is "correct." Thus, there is little need to provide a second such review. The intermediate court, therefore, is often in effect a court of last resort.

Intermediate courts have other important tasks. Chief among these is fleshing out high court doctrine and helping instruct trial courts in the application of case law, for the high court cannot generally do all that is necessary in this area. This duty requires of the intermediate court ungrudging understanding and application of what the court above has done; the intermediate court must also be willing to show where problems may be and alert the higher court to the need for correction. Here it is important that the lower court maintain credibility by not criticizing too often, saving its voice for what really matters; constructive criticism rather than carping or nit-picking should be the order of the day. The most important function of the intermediate appellate court, however, may be to screen cases. Screening saves the court above time and energy, for the opinion of the intermediate court helps separate out the important issues in the case, helping the court of last resort to concentrate on what is significant. In addition, the opinion of the intermediate court crystallizes thought of judges and counsel alike on those issues; that, in turn, can have an important effect on the quality of decision-making above.

§ 3.11   Appellate Review

The jurisdiction of appellate courts can be mandatory or discretionary. Generally, litigants, except in minor cases, are granted one appeal as of right; from a trial court of general jurisdiction (or an important administrative agency) the appeal often is to an intermediate appellate court. In a system with a large number of cases there may be no effective review of the work of the intermediate courts, for the court of last resort cannot take enough cases to review every decision that should be reviewed. Thus, in the federal system the Courts of Appeals are the effective end of the line because the Supreme Court can review only about 1% of the decisions of the Courts of Appeals each year.

Courts of last resort generally have two ways of obtaining jurisdiction over cases that entered the system elsewhere: mandatory and discretionary review.* These are important enough to be discussed separately.

a. Mandatory Review

Statutes often give aggrieved litigants a right of appeal. Busy courts, concerned with their caseload, have found formulae for avoiding full review or hearing under those statutes.

Oral argument may be dispensed with, for example, and the case decided on the record and briefs before it. (A professional legal staff may be involved in screening cases for the court, suggesting which cases should be given plenary consideration.) The payoff for the judges, of course, is the saving of time; on the other hand, that saving is arguably accomplished at the expense of the apparent legislative mandate. It is doubtful, however, that review mandated by statute has today any real justification, especially given the demands on the court's calendar; in many jurisdictions its continued existence seems simply to be an historical relic. Hence, some would argue that there is nothing wrong when a court bypasses the obligatory review process. It must be emphasized, however,

---

* A court of last resort may also obtain cases as part of its *original* jurisdiction. The Massachusetts Supreme Judicial Court, for example, issues advisory opinions to the state legislature when so requested by that body, or the United States Supreme Court decides disputes between states. Both forms of adjudication represent an exercise of power in a problem not previously heard by another court; those powers, therefore, are not part of the court's appellate jurisdiction. Such cases form a small part of the high court's docket.

that short-cuts can lead to problems. These will be discussed infra at § 4.19. In addition, the whole process can be abused.

In Snepp v. United States (1980), for example, the Supreme Court summarily affirmed, without oral argument, a holding that the CIA could censor a book written by a former employee. That decision, which was both controversial and important, has been widely criticized for having been made in that fashion.

b. *Discretionary Jurisdiction—Certiorari.*

The appellate jurisdiction of most intermediate appellate courts is mandatory—in theory they have no choice but to take the case. On the other hand, as the final appellate tribunals in a system, courts of last resort generally are not so bound. Typically, a large portion of their jurisdiction will be discretionary—that is, the courts themselves have the power to declare jurisdiction over the cases. That kind of review is often called "discretionary" because the courts have been given the power to choose the cases they review. Review by writ of certiorari comprises the largest portion of discretionary jurisdiction.

i. The Label. The practical effect of the "discretionary" label is that the court feels no obligation to explain its decision to grant (or not to grant) a petition for certiorari; thus a denial of "cert" will rarely be accompanied by explanation of that denial. "Practical considerations," Justice

Frankfurter once explained concerning a denial of certiorari, preclude such a course. Maryland v. Baltimore Radio Show, Inc. (1950). A court faced with a great number of petitions would find itself very hard-pressed indeed to explain each decision. Lack of a need to justify a decision has other perceived advantages, for it means that the court can decline to hear cases that it does not wish to hear. It may believe, for example, that although the case implicates an important "public" issue, the facts of the case may not present the legal issue clearly enough for effective decision-making. The court may also fear that counsel may not be equal to the task of properly delineating the issues for the court. Further, certiorari may be denied if the court believes that experience with the problem, especially in the lower courts, has been insufficient to crystallize thought (and possible solutions) to the problem; hence, the reviewing court may feel that the problem should "kick around" a bit longer before it attempts to impose a solution.

A more controversial reason for denying a petition would be a belief by the court that the issue is too emotion-laden or politically "hot" to handle at the time the petition is brought. In refusing to hear the case the court may believe that it is preserving precious political capital for other more important issues, or, indeed, for the preservation of the institutional strength of the court itself. An example of this process appears to be the consistent refusal of the Supreme Court to review cases challenging the constitutionality of the Vietnam

War. E.g., Mora v. McNamara (1967) (Justices Douglas and Stewart dissented from the denial).

Commentators are not agreed on the desirability of that practice. Alexander Bickel argued eloquently on behalf of widespread use of "passive virtues" such as denial of certiorari in order to preserve judicial power and prestige. Bickel, The Passive Virtues, 75 Harv.L.Rev. 40 (1961). Gerald Gunther, in The Subtle Vices of the "Passive Virtues"—A Comment on Principle and Expediency in Judicial Review, 64 Colum.L.Rev. 1 (1964), argued the other side just as strongly. Perhaps the most telling objection to Professor Bickel's theory made by Professor Gunther is the lack of any principled basis for its application. "Passive virtues" may cloak a clearly less permissible reason for not reviewing the case. On the other hand, that problem inheres in all forms of discretionary adjudication, including certiorari. Perhaps its continued existence and acceptance reflect our belief that we can tolerate some discretion, as long as it is not abused.

ii. Standards. Statutes and court rules rarely elaborate significantly on the general statement that the grant of certiorari is an act of discretion. Generally, the applicable rule will repeat that review is discretionary, and then state that review will be granted only when it is desirable or in the public interest to do so. See, e.g., Supreme Court Rule 19. The reluctance of courts to address systematically this question strongly suggests that courts of last resort do not wish to fetter their own discretion. In practice, however, more concrete guidance can be given. See generally R. Stern & E. Gressman, Supreme Court Practice Ch. 4, 6th ed. 1986, and the statement by Chief Justice Vinson, Work of the Federal Courts, 69 S.Ct. v-vi (1949). That kind of advice is important for the help it gives attorneys in drafting petitions, and the help it gives commentators who try to review a court's work.

How does a petitioner convince a court that the public would be served by granting the petition? First, she can argue that the rule in the case will affect a great many persons. Next, petitioner should show that the issue has not been previously decided by the Court; here it would be helpful if the lower courts were in conflict on the resolution of the issue (this last ground for review is at times specifically provided for). Failing that, petitioner may be able to show that the majority of other jurisdictions does things differently, or that there is a trend to that effect, or, at least, some criticism of the current rule. Always the petitioner has to keep the judges' minds on the fact that the case is one of those which, in Chief Justice Vinson's words, "present questions whose resolution will have immediate importance far beyond the particular facts and parties involved." Id. at vi.

An argument unlikely to be effective, in contrast, is that the court below erred, especially if that error affects no one other than the litigants. Courts of last resort are beseiged by petitions and they simply do not have the time to review for such errors. As Justice Stewart observed in Butz v. Glover Livestock Com'n Co., Inc. (1973) (dissenting):

> The only remarkable thing about this case is its presence in this Court. For the case involves no more than the application of well settled principles to a familiar situation, and has little significance except for the respondent. Why certiorari was granted is a mystery to me—particularly at a time when the Court is thought by many to be burdened by too heavy a caseload.

The Supreme Court grants a petition if four Justices believe the case "certworthy." The practice of requiring close to a majority decision to grant the petition probably is typical of most courts, for it is an effective way of controlling the court's docket. Occasionally, it will appear to a court after it has granted a petition that it had made a mistake in doing so—perhaps the petition had not correctly stated the situation, or circumstances have changed (e.g., a statute has been changed). The court will in those cases dismiss the petition for certiorari as "having been improvidently granted." The effect of that dismissal is the same as an initial denial of the petition.

iii. Effect of a Denial. A decision on a certiorari petition is not a decision on the merits. A petition can be denied for any reason whatever. Hence a certiorari decision is said to be "without precedential" value. See the opinions by Justice

Frankfurter in Maryland v. Baltimore Radio Show, supra, and by Justice Stevens in Singleton v. Commissioner (1978). The force of that very traditional statement has been undermined somewhat by two fairly recent phenomena on the Supreme Court, practices perhaps encountered on other courts as well.

The first is the habit of some Justices of issuing dissents from denials of certiorari. Such a dissent is likely to make the denial loom larger than it probably was meant to, for it suggests disagreement by the majority with the dissenter *on the merits*. A related problem with the dissent was pointed out by Justice Stevens in Huffman v. Florida (1978): " * * * a persuasive dissent may create the unwarranted impression that the Court has acted arbitrarily in denying a petition for certiorari."

A second practice diminishing the tradition that certiorari denials are non-precedential is that of explaining in some cases the reasons for the denial of certiorari. In Illinois v. Gray (1978), for example, the Court stated: "Certiorari denied, it appearing that the judgment below rests on an adequate state ground." Justice Stevens again noted his displeasure: "The Court's occasional practice of explaining its denials of certiorari is, I believe, inconsistent with the rule that such denials have no precedential value. Since I regard that rule as an important aspect of our practice, I do not join the Court's explanation in this case."

Despite those practices, no formal effort appears underway to change the no-precedent rule. A parting comment may be in order, however: It has always seemed doubtful that in any case of notoriety that the bar or public really believes that the court has not adjudicated—just a little bit, perhaps—on the merits of the dispute. That belief, however, does not square with doctrine.

c. *The Role of Counsel*

Lawyers play a major role in the appellate process. The briefs each side prepares provide the judges with a guide to the facts developed below, the arguments each believes to be relevant, and research on the issues. The briefs help *shape* the case by focusing attention on those facts and questions the lawyers believe to be important. The judges, of course, are not limited to the issues counsel raise, and often a court will strike off on a tangent of its own in order to decide a case. Nonetheless, the briefs do set the stage and provide the initial framework in which the court views the problem.

Oral argument presents counsel with an opportunity to engage the court; getting the judges interested in the case is a primary goal of any litigator. It also gives the judges a chance to clear up their own questions and to make sure they understand each party's position.

The role of counsel has diminished somewhat in recent years. Most jurisdictions now have an expedited appeal process which requires short briefs. More significant has been a trend away from oral argument. Many courts have adopted procedures which permit the case to be decided on "submission"—that is, on the written record (including the briefs); more than a third of the cases decided by the federal courts of appeals, for example, are decided on submission. These procedures save time and money for both the courts and the litigants; the cost lies in the risk that the shortcuts to decision-making will prevent the court from properly understanding the case.

d. The Role of Staff

Judges are not the only court personnel involved in the opinion process. There has been a marked increase in "para-judicial" staff in recent decades. These come in two general types: personal and staff clerks.

Most judges have at least one personal clerk (sometimes called an "elbow" clerk). Federal trial judges and many appellate judges have two clerks, and some appellate judges have more. Personal clerks have usually just graduated from law school, generally at the top of their class. Their job is to help the judge with research, to help write opinions, to recommend whether certiorari should be granted, and to do whatever else needs to be done in order to make the judge's office work better.

Most appellate courts now also have a central staff, some of which are quite large. The composition of the central staff varies widely; some are recent law school graduates who may leave after a year, others stay on for several years, and some view the position as a career. Central staff recommend whether argument should be heard in a case, help draft opinions, and solve problems which might arise in the appellate process. Central staff answer to the chief judge and to the court as a whole, rather than to an individual judge.

The increase in staff has led to a change in the way courts operate. No longer can decisions be thought to be the exclusive work of the judges themselves. Today's judge runs a small law office—several clerks, central staff, even student interns—and the decisions generally must be thought of as a product of that office. The judge supervises, of course, and often plays a major role, at least in important cases. But in minor cases and in other areas of decision-making—such as deciding whether to grant certiorari or to hear oral argument—staff play a large (and largely unacknowledged) role in today's appellate decision-making.

§ 3.12   The Role of the Trial Court

We tend to view the trial court's role in terms of its role in the fact-finding process, especially its relationship with the jury. That role is of extreme importance in the decision-making process, although beyond the scope of this *Nutshell.* The trial court, however, also plays a significant role in

the law making game. It is the court of first
instance where issues are initially formulated and
developed, where law is sought out and applied. In
performing those tasks the trial court uses the
same techniques as appellate courts. And if law is
not readily available, trial courts must develop
principles to cover the situation.

The pressure of caseload necessarily makes it
more difficult for the trial judge to perform those
tasks in the way that appellate courts can. The
court's attention must often be directed to a large
number of issues in each case, further limiting its
ability to handle individual issues in depth. The
basic task of any court remains, however, to do
justice and provide law.

CHAPTER FOUR
COMMON LAW ADJUDICATION
PART A
THE GOALS
§ 4.1 Overview

This Chapter of the *Nutshell* examines the manner in which judges decide cases in which the decision is not controlled either by a statute (the superior demand of the legislature) or a constitution (organic law), but instead reflects their own views of what the law should be.

The Chapter begins by reaching a working definition of law and of the goals of adjudication. There follows a discussion of precedent—what it is, how it works, and when it should control a decision. Next, the problem of creation of precedent will be examined—how, why, and when it is done. Finally, the problem of overruling will be discussed.

§ 4.2 Jurisprudence—An Overview

The nature of law is a problem that has occupied the attention of humanity for millenia. It will be useful to sketch very briefly the major schools of thought. One believes that law—or its sources—

exists independently of human thought or endeavor. Such "Natural Law" may be grounded in theology or in philosophy. Among the great names associated with this school are Aquinas, Locke, Rousseau, and Kant.

Other thinkers reject the existence of a higher law. Some believe law to be merely the specific application of the historical or customary behavior of a people. The "historical" school is associated most closely with Savigny, Maine, and, in this country, a lawyer named James Carter. Still others have rejected, as it were, the notion that law has any "source," and concentrated their attention on law as simply the authoritative command of the state. The most famous of these "positivists" is a nineteenth century English judge, John Austin; the most famous American, a professor, John Chipman Gray. One manifestation of positivism, popular among judges and scholars in the generation before World War I, was an excessive preoccupation with rules, so-called "black-letter" law.

Disbelief in natural law, however, does not lead necessarily to lack of concern with the content of the law. Many influential writers have spoken of the goals that law seeks to achieve. Among these are utilitarians such as Jeremy Bentham and an American school of "Sociological Jurisprudence" led by Dean Roscoe Pound and Judge (later Justice) Benjamin Cardozo, a group sometimes joined by Justice Holmes. The goals sought by those thinkers cover the range of human experience.

In 1930 a new school, "Legal Realism," set up shop. Building on the recognition that law serves social ends, the Realists argued that judges largely ignored "rules" and sought to achieve what they perceived as justice. Hence, the focus of scholarly inquiry, the Realists argued, should be on what judges actually do, including the uncertain methods used in "judging," rather than on analysis of substantive rules. The Realists were led by Professors Karl Llewellyn and Jerome Frank (later a judge).

Following World War II a reaction to realist jurisprudence set in as first Professors Henry Hart and Albert Sacks and then Karl Llewellyn showed how the standards of craftsmanship imposed by the common law tradition shaped the judicial process and limited the "freedom" of judges to do as they wished. The two major works were Llewellyn's The Common Law Tradition: Deciding Appeals (1960), and Hart and Sacks, The Legal Process: Basic Problems in the Making and Application of Law (1958). (The latter work, labeled a "tentative" edition by its authors, has never been "finished"; nevertheless, it is a widely used casebook in American law schools and has been enormously influential—it has given its name to the "Legal Process" school of jurisprudence.)

A number of influential attacks have been made on the Legal Process school in the past two or three decades. Some have criticized it as naive, for failing to recognize the role economic and political pressure groups play in the legislative and judicial process. Others have argued that Legal Process jurisprudence really reflects the tacit assumptions of its proponents and of the ruling elite they largely represent; the views of others are not heard or needed. Still others believe that the efforts of the Legal Process adherents are really a cloak for ad hoc and unprincipled decision-making, that their efforts to limit discretion and channel decision-making are at best illusory. These criticisms have been strong at times; nevertheless, the great majority of judges write opinions that accept legal process as the proper guide to decision-making. The continued acceptance of that methodology is not surprising. It does provide judges with a method of determining in a relatively neutral and predictable fashion what the law should be.

Many other jurisprudential movements could be mentioned. Three of recent importance are law and economics, critical legal studies, and feminism. The law and economics school, associated principally with Judge Richard Posner (formerly Professor), evaluates legal issues according to a cost-benefit analysis; this analysis can be used for many, or even all, legal issues. A critical legal studies movement, led by Professors Duncan Kennedy and Robert Unger, began in the early eighties. Its goal was to examine ("critically") the underlying assumptions of every legal rule—especially the tacit assumptions concerning social structure. The feminist school, associated with Professors Catherine MacKinnon and Robin West, questioned the neutrality and universality of legal doctrine, and argued that the law has largely excluded the perceptions and experiences of women.

§ 4.3 Law—A Working Definition

Exploration of those schools—much less their resolution—is far beyond the scope of this work. Law can be defined satisfactorily for our purposes in a less ambitious way, for Anglo–American lawyers and judges generally use the term to express one of two meanings. First, "law" is used in a positivist fashion to refer to an authoritative statement (that is, one backed by the power of the state) concerning something that has happened; if, for example, a court decides that defendant owes plaintiff $25,000 for breach of contract then "law" has been applied to that situation. (This does not mean other "law" might not also be applicable— the "law of God," for example—but common lawyers do not normally so express themselves.) Law as command does not, of course, come only from courts. In American jurisprudence, the primary law comes from the federal and state constitutions and, within its proper sphere, from the legislature.

The second meaning of law looks forward in time: "Law", Holmes told us, "is merely, a prediction of what judges will do." Holmes, The Path of the Law, 10 Harv.L.Rev. 457 (1897). When used in that fashion law provides a guide for future conduct, a method of predicting possible consequences of action yet contemplated, or of action performed but whose legal effect has not yet been determined. "Law," in short, resolves past problems and guides action still to come.

§ 4.4   A Word on Justice

Law and justice seem to some to bear only a fortuitous relationship. Ideology and law, some would argue, cannot be separated. That may well be. To one trained in the common law, however, law and justice are inseparable. "Equal justice under law" reads the inscription on the entablature of the Supreme Court, reminding us that justice in our system is not dispensed on an individualized, *ad hoc* basis. It comes, instead, equally to all who are similarly situated.

Other definitions of justice are easy to come by. But in the common law, at least, "the law is no respecter of persons." Or, as the oath of office for federal judges puts it: "I will administer justice without respect to persons, and do equal right to the poor and rich * * *." 28 U.S.C.A. § 453.

§ 4.5   The Goals of Judicial Decision Making

The following suggests some goals to be sought by the adjudicative process.

a.   *Finality*

The court should to the extent possible dispose of the case before it; the authoritative resolution of the dispute should be clear and intelligible. To insure finality a host of ancillary doctrines such as law of the case, res judicata, and collateral estoppel have been invented; they will not be developed in this book.

b. Efficiency

The system should operate efficiently to accomplish its goals.

c. Social Goals

The articulation of much of American law has been left to the judiciary. For that reason the decision should seek to establish legal rules that help advance the many goals of our society. When deciding a case, in other words, the court should decide which of society's goals will be involved in the decision and how they can best be furthered.

d. Stability

Society seeks a large mixture of substantive goals. In addition to achieving those substantive ends, however, stability in expectations must be considered as an extremely important end in itself. Stability reduces uncertainty and thus helps all those who come in contact with decisional law— e.g., prosecutors, business, labor unions—to plan their activities with a minimum of risk. Thus, stability is a very important end for the adjudicative process to seek.

e. Fairness

The goals of stability, finality, and substantive accomplishment are important, but their achievement must also accommodate fairness, a term that encompasses at least two meanings. The first is justice in the sense of reaching decisions that do not conflict with moral values.

Fairness also involves an assurance of fair dealing by the court. Justice cannot be fully satisfied without an opinion that explains the manner in which the decision was reached, and why it is consistent with past decisions. That explanation helps make the decision fair, for it assures the parties that they have been treated fairly, that the court has paid attention to their claims of right, has thought about those claims, and has rejected them for good reasons.

It is perhaps unrealistic to ask a losing litigant to accept the judgment as fair. But it is very important that anyone else coming into contact with the decision believe it to be fair. Without that appearance of fairness, the confidence in the system so necessary to its continued success cannot be maintained.

§ 4.6 The Reasoned Opinion

Those goals can best be achieved in an opinion that explains why the court reached the results it did in the case at bar. That requirement comes down to us from of old. Two centuries ago a

Parliamentary committee reported that "no positive law" compelled judges "to give a reasoned opinion from the bench, in support of their judgments upon matters that are stated before them. But the course has prevailed from the oldest times. It has been so general and so uniform that it must be considered the law of the land." *Quoted in* P. Brest, Processes of Constitutional Decision Making 1088 (1975). A number of state constitutions make the same point, for they mandate that decisions— at least of the highest court—state the basis of the decision.

Why that requirement? First, a reasoned opinion is necessary to provide an effective basis for review by a higher tribunal. Although this observation is generally made in the context of administrative decisions, it applies equally to judicial decisions. Rule 52(a) of the Federal Rules of Civil Procedure, for example, mandates that a court trying a case without a jury "set forth the findings of fact and conclusions of law which constitute the grounds of its action." The point, of course, is that a reviewing court will have a great deal of difficulty in doing its job if the court below has not explained its reasoning. Consider a breach of contract action based on an alleged contract where the defendant asserts two defenses: no contract was formed, and even if one had been formed it was discharged due to impracticability. A mere statement of "judgment for defendant" simply provides no help to the reviewing court, for it deprives that body of the insight by the trial judge—who was closer to the case—as to why defendant should win. Similarly, a decision that reads "judgment for plaintiff" is unsatisfactory, for it does not tell the higher court why the defenses were rejected.

A related goal of the written opinion requirement is to provide a check on arbitrary decision-making. In part, appellate review serves that function, but it is very important that such review come from sources outside the judiciary—from the bar, the public, and from scholars. Even if those groups do not in fact review particular decisions— and of course that is largely the case—the possibility of their doing so may help check arbitrary decision-making. Those groups face the same problem as an appellate court, however, for if explanation has not been offered, review has been made impossible.

Reasoned opinions also make it easier to understand what the law *is*; a reasoned explanation of why the court came out the way it did contributes a great deal to an understanding of what the court will do in analogous situations. Underscoring the importance of this function of the elaborated decision is recognition of the fact that much of legal reasoning is by analogy, a process greatly helped by an opinion that tries to explain why the court reached the result that it did and the policies the court sought to implement.

A final explanation for the reasoned opinion requirement comes from the value of the judge's exploration—for himself, in writing, for review by a critical audience—of his own analytic processes. Richard Wasserstrom, in his illuminating book, The Judicial Decision (1961), called this the "process of justification", one that insures that the opinion is as accurate as possible, and the conduct undertaken as beneficial as possible. Thus, the requirement of a reasoned opinion also tries to force a judge to "think," rather than merely to "react," in order best to explain the decision to the public. Wasserstrom differentiated what he styled "the process of discovery" from that of justification. The distinction is important, for it focuses attention on the need to articulate and explain a result, no matter how that result was "discovered." Many judges have testified that this process does, in fact, work, and that there are occasions when an opinion simply "won't write." When that happens, of course, the course of the law can take a dramatic new form. "A judge must do more than decree," Judge Roger Traynor wrote, "he must reason every inch of the way." The Limits of Judicial Creativity, 29 Hastings L.Rev. 1025 (1978).

The value of the justification process is lost, of course, if the judge does not pay attention in good faith to the value of the justification he comes up with. At times, that does not seem to be the case; as every law student knows, many opinions do not hold together on careful reading. Much of that can be traced to human error, for most judges do pay close attention to the quality of their opinions. Karl Llewellyn, in his great book, The Common Law Tradition (supra, § 4.2), discussed a number of factors that limit the possibility that the judge will ignore the results of the "process of justification". Those factors center on the craft expectations of those trained in the "common law tradition," one that does emphasize the importance of using reason to illuminate the path to the decision.

My own belief is similar to Llewellyn's. Almost all judges work well within the tradition and try not to sell a result that they believe cannot be supported on solid grounds. Granting readily that pre-conceived notions influence the valuations required by the justification process, I would still argue the reasoned opinion serves to limit the ability of an opinion-writer to give effect to those notions.

The "process of justification" is not simply an individual process; it should also occur among the judges of an appellate court. As Henry Hart observed, the circulation of draft opinions, of critiques, of formal and informal conferences, should lead to a "maturing of collective thought." Hart, The Time Chart of the Justices, 73 Harv.L.Rev. 84, 100 (1959). Some have doubted whether those processes really work; attempts to utilize them can also be viewed as efforts, for better or worse, to rationalize a decision already arrived at on the basis of deeply held convictions. See the debate among Professor Hart, id.; Thurman Arnold (who was both a professor and judge), Professor Hart's Theology, 73 Harv.L.Rev. 1298 (1960); and Dean Erwin Griswold, Of Time and Attitudes—Professor

Hart and Judge Arnold, 74 Harv.L.Rev. 81 (1969). That debate, of course, can never be resolved. Ample examples can be found, however, of instances where courts have changed the shape of the opinion, or even the result in the case, following the circulation of draft opinions.

§ 4.7 Some More on Reasoning

Students of the goals of opinion writing have come up with a number of terms that help explain the process. It will be useful to discuss briefly three of them: reasoned elaboration, neutral principles, and mechanical jurisprudence.

a. Reasoned Elaboration

Hart and Sacks (supra, § 4.2) coined this phrase to express their view of the duty of an opinion writer. An opinion that satisfied their standard justified the conclusions that it reached by the use of reasoning that sets forth carefully and cogently the manner in which the decision was reached. Further, reasoned elaboration requires that the judge strive for consistency between the opinion and related views in other cases. The opinion must also be written in a way that is most likely to fulfill the policies that it identifies. The phrase "reasoned elaboration" has become famous and is often used today when talking about the need for a judge to outline carefully the steps that explain the decision reached by the court. "Reasoned elaboration" reflects a belief that because law is purposive it must be developed in rational terms. Doing so helps the court's audience see the goals identified by the court, its method of reaching those goals, and permits criticism of opinions using the same bases.

b. Neutral Principles

In a famous essay critical of then-current decision-making on the Supreme Court, Herbert Wechsler argued that judges should decide cases through the generation of "neutral principles." Wechsler, Toward Neutral Principles of Constitutional Law, 73 Harv.L.Rev. 1 (1959). Wechsler defined a "neutral principle" as one that a judge would be willing to apply in all cases covered by the principle formulated by the court. A "neutral principle" must also be general enough to cover cases other than those factually identical to the one at bar, and it must be based upon policies sound enough to justify its existence.

Neutral Principles created something of a furor when it was published, partly due to its criticism of the opinion in Brown v. Board of Educ. (1954). Critics argued that judges should be free to do "good" even if established law did not permit the "good" result and the court was not willing to change that law. They also contended that a court, as a political institution, should be free to maximize its political impact by manipulating its opinions to that end. Finally, some read Wechsler as suggesting that there were such things as "neutral" principles akin to natural law, although he used the term to mean that a court should be prepared to use a principle in all cases where its policy would lead it to be applied.

The phrase "neutral principles" has become part of our tradition. The article of that name should be read by all students of common-law decision-making.

c. Decision by Pigeonhole: Maxims, Magic Words, and Mechanical Jurisprudence

A common trap for any court is to react to a situation presented it for decision by placing it automatically in a pigeonhole, without thought to the implications of doing so. A court cannot redo from scratch every issue in every case presented to it for decision (a fact more true of trial courts than of appellate ones), but on the key issues its duty is, to the extent possible, to approach the solution with a questioning mind: Is this a good rule, what are its consequences, how well does existing law on point work given developments in other fields? The court must always be seeking fresh solutions to old problems.

That may not be as easy as it appears. A judge's mind can easily become full of pigeonholes. After all, most of the problems *are* repetitive, and often counsel provide none of the insight needed to stimulate a new look. Further, when problems have already been dealt with the mind tends to react in a way that will save the effort already expended in analysis of the problem. A court must constantly be on the alert against mental laziness. The decision suggested by habit may not necessarily be the right one.

Writing at the beginning of this century, Dean Roscoe Pound warned of judges who suffered from this problem and who wrote opinions that reflected what he styled "mechanical jurisprudence," a style that relied heavily on the incantation of "magic words," rather than on analysis of the problem to reach a decision. Pound, Mechanical Jurisprudence, 8 Colum.L.Rev. 605 (1908). Judges who engaged in mechanical jurisprudence wrote opinions that pursued a legal doctrine or maxim to a logical extreme "with relentless disregard of consequences," as Cardozo explained in Hynes v. New York Central R.R. Co. (1921). Judge Braxton Craven called such judges "sterile" judges, an excellent phrase. Paean to Pragmatism, 50 N.C.L.Rev. 977 (1972).

It is of course easy (and therefore tempting) to decide a case by labeling it with a time honored maxim. "Danger invites rescue" and "instinct with obligation," two phrases from the New York Court of Appeals, illustrate the ability of maxims to capture vividly a problem and suggest a solution from the stored wisdom of society (see the discussion in § 5.17 of the analogous problem of canons of construction in statutory interpretation). But that once thought wise may no longer be so. In tort and contract law, for example, vast changes in doctrine have been brought about in the past two generations by judges who did not react mechanically to problems; examples are strict liability, comparative negligence, promissory estoppel, and commercial impracticability.

Serious problems can arise, however, when judges do not devote fresh thought to a problem. No area illustrates this better than that of choice of law (a subject dealing with which law to apply to a legal dispute which touches more than one state). For several generations American conflicts law operated on a territorial principle; in a tort action, for example, the law where the cause of action arose was applied. Many problems arose, however, that the territorial approach did not solve: where *does* a cause of action arise—where the negligent act took place, where the trauma occurred, or where the injury was discovered? How does a court even know if a "tort" or a "contract" is involved? These were not very difficult questions to answer in the "easy" cases, but trouble often arose when the question was close, for the territorial approach to conflicts adjudication was not rooted in a systematic evaluation of the goals of the various laws that might be applied. The absence of such an evaluation meant that it was impossible to answer hard questions in a consistent fashion. Instead decision-making often appeared to be *ad hoc* and, indeed, to frustrate many of the substantive policies implicated by the problem.

Beginning in the 1960's, however, courts, building on the work of scholars, rejected the mechanical approach to conflicts represented by the territorialists. Today's conflicts problems are generally evaluated in the light of an analytic appreciation of the policies underlying the rules that might be applied to the problem—a shift in doctrine to a decidedly non-mechanical jurisprudence.

The dangers of mechanical jurisprudence are not limited to the doctrinal level. Even when the substance of the law is satisfactory, thought must be carefully given before uttering magic words. In contract law, for example, certain consequences follow upon the labeling of a condition in an agreement as precedent or subsequent. The significance of that label is to allocate the burden of proof as to whether the condition occurred. Thus, the real question before the court in those cases is which of the parties should be allocated that burden. Once that question has been answered, then, and only then, should the label be placed on the problem. The important thing is to think in terms of reasons and results, rather than in labels and concepts.

§ 4.8 Do Hard Cases Make Bad Law?

In Winterbottom v. Wright (1842), Baron Rolfe uttered one of the more famous legal aphorisms: "Hard cases, it has been frequently observed, make bad law." That quote, usually written without the middle clause, has been much used in the century and a half since it was uttered. It is usually taken to mean that a court faced with a particularly appealing set of facts (e.g., widows and orphans oppressed by vicious mortgagees) and decisional law that oppresses the deserving, "cheats" its way to a result. The "hard case"—evicting widows and orphans—has made "bad law" because the opinion is also a precedent that may not work well with the structure of existing law. Our courts, on the other hand, do not generally articulate a belief that they sit to do justice only between the parties before them. In our system justice requires that law be applied with an even hand. It is no accident that the figure of Justice is normally portrayed blindfolded, a belief captured in the observation, "The law is no respecter of persons." Law should not be skewed simply because one side is thought evil or bad. We do not throw out an otherwise valid contract between bank and widow simply because the widow's case appeals more to our sense of fair play. Some courts have displayed a good deal of pride with respect to the rigor of their approach. An oft-cited example is Gluck v. Baltimore (1895), in which the court displayed great fortitude: "Obviously a principle, if sound, ought to be applied wherever it logically leads, without reference to ulterior results. That it may, in consequence, operate in some instances with apparent, or even with real, harshness and severity, does not indicate that it is inherently erroneous. Its consequence in special cases can never impeach its accuracy."

This is not to say that the widow and orphan should have no effect on the law. Indeed, their plight should be a signal to the court that the substance of the law in this area may need rethinking. An example of that rethinking can be found in the development in contract law of methods to soften the impact of the doctrine that express conditions must be complied with literally. To avoid problems of fairness associated with breach near the end of the contract term, the doctrines of immaterial breach and substantial performance developed; problems associated with non-performance acquiesced in by the non-breaching party led to the doctrine of waiver. In this way the law changed as the courts coped with the problems of "hard cases." Similarly, contract law has developed doctrines such as duress and unconscionability to protect the widow who contracts with the bank.

The hard case problem thus is linked with that of mechanical jurisprudence. A court faced with a distasteful result must come to grips with the problem. It may be that the court was right in *Gluck* and uniformity and consistency exact a high price at times. But it may also be that the dilemma posed by the hard case in fact represents a challenge to the court to help the law accommodate different societal interests. At the very least it may help the court avoid the cardinal sin of mechanical decision-making.

§ 4.9 Opinion Style

During the two centuries of our existence as a nation judges have written opinions in many different styles. At present, the generally accepted model requires a statement of the history of the case, a recital of facts, presentation of issues to be decided, resolution of those issues, and an explanation of why those issues were so resolved. Once past that outline, styles vary widely. Some judges are verbose, tracing the history of every doctrine back to the Year Books, while others are terse. The quality of reasoning also varies widely. Some judges, content to rely on authority found in the Restatement, in treatises, and in precedents, do not reexamine underlying issues. Others probe deeply, reasoning carefully, examining each issue as if seeing it for the first time. All, however, believe it necessary to justify the decision in some fashion.

A number of scholars have argued that the styles and type of reasoning in opinions at different periods of our history resulted from the way individual judges viewed their role in the formation of the law. Karl Llewellyn, (supra, § 4.2), spoke of the "Grand Style" of the great common law judges like Shaw of Massachusetts and Gibson of Pennsylvania (roughly 1825–1860), who authored opinions that broke with the past openly, though retaining continuity with it. Their opinions were refreshing inquiries into the reasonableness of particular results, often relying little on precedent but always relying on reasoning. Lemuel Shaw's opinion in Norway Plains Co. v. Boston & Maine R.R. (1854), perhaps exemplifies this best. In *Norway Plains* the court was asked to hold that the long-established rule of strict liability for common carriers should be applied to railroads. Shaw's opinion cites but a handful of cases and relies on none for the holding. Instead, the judge examined the question by referring to the contractual expectations of the parties in light of the differences between railroads and other common carriers.

The Grand Style, according to Llewellyn, died out following the Civil War, and was replaced by a style that relied on formalism. Opinions at the end of the nineteenth century were prolix and over-laden with citation. A great deal of reliance was placed on maxims. The opinions give the reader the impression that the outcome was inevitable, and that the judge's role did not encompass inquiry into the consequences of decisions in particular cases. Precedent, in short, was all.

Scholars debate what caused this shift, or even if it occurred. Certainly not all judges in either era behaved in accord with the paradigm. It is difficult to read opinions from the two eras, however, without recognizing that their flavor, at least, has changed markedly several times during our history.

§ 4.10   A Note on Name–Calling

Phrases such as "mechanical jurisprudence," or "neutral principles" can themselves easily become "magic words" applied to decisions by critics who think a judge may be too careful, for example, in maintaining links with the past. Those who believe, on the other hand, that a judge is moving too rapidly may use a sobriquet such as "judicial activist" to express displeasure with that course of action. It is not possible to please all of the people all of the time. Recognition of the possibility of using a phrase such as "mechanical jurisprudence" for rhetorical purposes, should not obscure its value in suggesting how judges should construct their opinions and approach their tasks.*

* Professor William Richman, who suggested the title of this section, has prepared a chart to help in choosing the appropriate epithet:

GUIDE TO JURISPRUDENTIAL NAMECALLING

	Decision is closely reasoned. All premises of legal syllogism are accepted. Statutory or decisional "rules"	Decision Loosely Reasoned. Premises depend on: (1) Analogy to similar fact patterns (2) Truths of history, sociology, etc. (3) Custom
I like the result	Strict Constructionism Judicial Restraint	The Grand Style Judicial Creativity
I dislike the result	Mechanical Jurisprudence The Formal Style	Judicial Irresponsibility Intellectual Dishonesty

PART B
PRECEDENT

§ 4.11   Stare Decisis

Our system of case law embodies the doctrine of precedent. An ancient doctrine, with roots as far back as the Year Books, it tells us that cases should be decided today the same way they were decided in the past. Another name for this doctrine is *stare decisis* (from a longer maxim, *stare decisis et non quieta movera*). As *stare decisis* is applied in American courts today, it is expected, in the event an apparently similar case is not followed, that the court explain why the precedent did not control (this is "distinguishing" the precedent; see § 4.16). Finally, the court may overrule the precedent, but again it must justify that decision. Although our courts do not adhere to a rigid view of *stare decisis*, that doctrine exerts a very strong force.

As might be expected of a doctrine of such distinguished lineage, *stare decisis* has many virtues. They can be broken down into three groups: efficiency, predictability, and uniformity or fairness.

—*Efficiency.* Precedent helps judges operate with more efficiency than would be the case if each issue not clearly covered by a statute had to be litigated from scratch in every case. Earlier decisions provide a quick reference for the judicial solution of present problems.

—*Predictability.* Judicial reliance on earlier decisions helps make the legal setting of any problem more predictable. An attorney drafting a contract, for example, is assured by the likelihood that prior rulings on liquidated damage clauses will be followed. Predictability reduces the risk associated with all the myriad activities of life that may end up in litigation. Reduction of risks enables society to operate more efficiently and is, therefore, a goal earnestly to be sought.

Predictability also reduces the amount of litigation. When problems arise, suit is less likely if the parties know the likely outcome. This encourages settlement, keeps cases out of court, and saves valuable social resources.

—*Uniformity.* By treating alike litigants who have similar problems, *stare decisis* insures uniform treatment. Uniformity is an essential element of fairness. The need to explain why an apparent precedent was not followed (the need for consistency in decision-making) makes it less likely that decisions will be based on arbitrary or impermissible criteria such as race, political connections, or the flip of a coin. Beyond that, the need to have similar cases decided similarly seems to be an indispensable component of our general belief in justice; if that belief is not supported, confidence in the judiciary will be undermined.

The virtues of *stare decisis,* of course, help to achieve most of the goals of adjudication described in § 4.5. *Stare decisis,* however, does have its drawbacks. The most important is a loss of flexibility, both in terms of the content of substantive law, and in the ability of a court to do "justice" between the parties only, as a philosopher-king might. We have responded to the first problem by permitting case law to change and grow over time, and by the occasional overruling of precedent. Those methods also help achieve some measure of the second kind of flexibility.

—*Bibliography.* There are a small number of quality discussions of *stare decisis.* The best is Karl Llewellyn's classic, The Bramble Bush (2d ed. 1951); see also the sources discussed in § 1.2, supra.

§ 4.12 Precedent and Judicial Power

The idea that judges can, through their opinions, bind themselves and their successors has been criticized by some Europeans on the ground that a system where judges are bound by their own decisions, as opposed to one where judges are not so bound, gives judges too much power. (Professor John Dawson's The Oracles of the Law (1961), is a good discussion of the topic.) Although it is true that the creation of precedent represents an exercise of judicial power, it is an exercise that seems to be successful, and one with which our society feels comfortable. The point, of course, is that the judge has power and her job requires that she use it; the real question is whether the power has been used properly.

Further, it can be argued that a system based on precedent gives judges *less* freedom than the Continental system in which judges are not formally bound by their decisions. Our judges have *less* freedom because our system imposes on them the need to decide like cases in like fashion. Common law judges lack the power, in other words, to decide as they see fit *in each case;* instead, they must be sure that every decision fits into the existing legal framework or explain why that framework is being changed. This limitation on judicial freedom is the fundamental accommodation between the need to make law and at the same time limit the exercise of power by the (often) non-elected judiciary.

§ 4.13 Scope of Precedent

The rule of *stare decisis* tells us that each judicial decision in our legal system is a "precedent" (except for certain unpublished opinions; see § 3.9). It "stands for" or "holds" something that generally controls future decisions. Unfortunately, courts and commentators have not agreed on how best to determine what that "something" is.

a. Some Theories

The common law has defined the force of *stare decisis* in a number of ways. Conventional wisdom has it that the *ratio decidendi* of a case, that is, the principle or rule of law laid down by the decision and *necessary* to the resolution of the case, contains the precedential effect of the decision. An example in an action brought by an appliance store against a consumer would be a statement that an unconscionable "contract" cannot be enforced. That establishes a rule that, when applied to the facts, disposes of the action. Some writers and judges, however, have urged that the precedential effect of a decision should be defined differently. An extreme view would be that the binding effect of a case is limited to the bare decision on the facts in the case. (Simply, "Agreements identical to this one cannot be enforced.") A more popular definition would find the binding effect in the facts of the case that the court stated were necessary to the decision. ("Agreements made by poor persons that contain certain pernicious clauses cannot be enforced.") A variant on this position urges that it is up to a later court to determine what facts were "necessary" to the decision. ("Although our predecessors emphasized the poverty of the consumer, it seems clear to us that what *really* motivated their decision was the consumer's lack of bargaining power.") Another view suggests that the binding effect of a precedent is to be found in the reasoning used to reach the decision. ("Freedom of contract is fine for persons of equal bargaining power, but when that power is not equal courts must protect the consumer from unconscionable sellers.") Finally, others have argued that the scope of a precedent cannot be correctly determined until the case has been interpreted and applied by later courts. Because later courts possess the advantage of hindsight, they can work with the precedent, restating its lessons as experience and commentary help them understand the problem better, so that the precedent may in the end stand for something different than it did in the beginning. (An example of this process is given in § 4.17.)

Perhaps it would be possible to define exactly what a precedent is and the weight that should be attached to it. That effort would not be fruitful, however, for it mistakes the values that case law brings to our society. Rather than try to analyze a decision through application of a tight definition of what a precedent *is,* the analysis should center on the goals of *stare decisis.* The analysis of precedent, in short, should be *functional.*

It should be easy to see why that is so and why American judges and scholars have not spent a great deal of effort in trying to define with precision the exact scope of a precedent. There is little need for that kind of precision in judicial systems such as ours that have no formal prohibitions against modifying or overruling decisions. An opinion represents a court's attempt to solve problems brought before it, and to explain to its audience why that solution was believed proper for that and similar cases (including what makes cases "similar"), to help those who read the opinion understand the decision in the present case and its future application. Thus, the importance of an opinion inheres in what it teaches its audience and how that audience responds to it. That is why all precedents must be evaluated in light of the several goals of *stare decisis*.

b. Further Analysis

Recognition of the need to evaluate precedent functionally helps us understand how to evaluate the force and sweep of a particular decision. To begin with, uniform decision-making requires that all similar cases be decided the same way. At the simplest level, then, the precedent is the decision itself. Strongly supporting that position is recognition of the fact that judicial power to make law comes only from the necessity of deciding cases. Yet analysis cannot stop there if the precedent is to control like cases. To determine similarity, a court must compare facts to see if the cases differ materially. Because cases can always be said to present different facts ("the consumer in the case at bar is a law student, the one in the earlier case was uneducated"), the court must determine whether any legal significance attaches to that difference. That search requires the later court to try to apply the rule of law laid down earlier. In order to do that properly, the second court must first read the rule in light of the facts that were deemed important to the decision by the precedent-setting court. (In our running unconscionability example, the earlier decision may have stressed the consumer's lack of education, thereby making that status a key inquiry.) It must do so because these facts show the problem to which the earlier court was responding. Of course, the opinion may not have exposed clearly what facts were deemed significant and a later court may make that determination for itself. ("Although not stressed in the earlier opinion, it seems clear to us that the decision was motivated not by the consumer's lack of education, but rather by his poverty.") This process is common enough. Hindsight may well help a later court understand that the earlier recitation did not accurately reflect the earlier court's thought processes; an opinion, after all, is written by humans who may express their thoughts imperfectly in writing. The later court, therefore, must be ready to re-evaluate the determination of what are "key" facts.

Beyond decision and facts lies the rule articulated by the precedent-setting court. The rule ("unfair agreements between persons of unequal bargaining power will not be enforced") is necessary for the judicial system to achieve its goals of consistency and predictability. It is the formulation of that rule to which the facts and decision point, and it is the rule that, perhaps more than any other factor in the precedent, is relied upon by others. The actual rule laid down in the case, therefore, is of great importance in determining the scope of a precedent.

Finally, the force of the precedent can also be found in the policies advanced by the court to justify its rule. It is those policies (explanations) that help fit the rule into the mainstream of the law. More important, a court cannot determine what facts were important or necessary to the decision, or decide whether a rule should be applied to a new set of facts, *unless* the reasons why the earlier case was decided are known. The inquiry into whether the reasons behind the earlier decision would be furthered by its application in the case at bar is the only way a court can determine whether the rule controls the later case. Thus, the policies that the rule seeks to achieve, along with the rule itself, the decision, and the facts, induce reliance and expectations and help promote understanding of what the precedent-setting court was trying to accomplish. For that reason, all of those elements must be considered in order to understand the precedent. To put this differently, the "conventional wisdom" and alternatives about precedent sketched briefly in the preceding subsection are *all* correct—partially—in their view of how to determine the scope of a precedent. All of the factors discussed there help a reader understand what the earlier court was trying to do—and what a later court *will* do (or, at least, is likely to do).

c. Some Other Considerations

A later court might examine the precedent in light of factors that influence the weight to be accorded it. Not all precedents, after all, are equal. Because they come in different packages each must be separately evaluated to determine the weight it should carry. Is an opinion, for example, from a system with wide influence (e.g., California), or from a well respected judge (e.g., Wald, Traynor, Edwards)? If so, it is likely to have more national influence, a fact that may influence both lawyers and judges. Is the case from a state with similar problems in the area? (A decision on riparian rights from a desert state such as Nevada would probably be more influential in another dry state than would one from, say, Florida.) Is the opinion the work of a high court or of a trial court? Did the court speak with one voice or was the decision fragmented into a number of different opinions? Above all else, how well *reasoned* is the opinion: How well did the court justify the decision that it reached by arguing the desirability of the policies that it sought to implement and explain how the decision furthered them? Each of those factors influences the magnitude of the precedent; that is, the degree to which it will influence a later court.

The later history of a precedent, as courts have applied or distinguished it, must also be considered a measure of the precedent's scope. The process is one both of correction and of evolution. Correction occurs because an opinion, for example, may state a rule less than happily. After all, judges are human, and language does not operate with mathematical precision. It then becomes necessary to modify language used earlier to express the court's solution better. The evolution of a precedent is also important. A later court may believe that the earlier court covered too much territory in its opinion, and that the precedent actually stands for something more narrow than is suggested by the phrasing of the opinion. Equally likely, perhaps, the precedent may have been phrased too narrowly. In each of these situations the precedent needs to be recast by a later court. The court's initial reaction to a problem represents a groping towards an imperfectly perceived goal. "It is the merit of the common law," Holmes argued, "that it decides the case first and determines the principle afterwards." Holmes, Codes and The Arrangement of Law, 5 Am.L.Rev. 1 (1870).

Unfortunately, courts all too often fail to *evaluate* precedent. Instead, any case, no matter how poorly reasoned it may be, sometimes seems ripe for use as authority if it can be said to have a holding akin to the one the present court is seeking to justify.

The need to evaluate the teachings of precedent does not mean that a later court can do as it wishes with earlier cases. Limits exist beyond which a precedent cannot fairly be narrowed or expanded. A case may teach many things, but it cannot be turned on its head. One limitation on the scope of precedent is found in the distinction between the *holding* of the case and the *dictum*.

§ 4.14 Dictum

A statement in a case that is not necessary to the decision is said to be *dictum*. *Dicta* are not considered to be part of the precedent. (Remember that judicial power to make law arises from the necessity of *deciding* cases.)

The difficulty of determining the scope of a decision's precedential force suggests that a search for *dicta* may not be very helpful. The term can become a derogatory label, used by lawyers writing briefs, judges writing opinions, and professors bedevilling students, to discredit an inconvenient or disliked part of a decision. One perceptive student writer, noting the difficulties in defining and applying the term, concluded that designating part of a case as *dictum* is primarily a shorthand method of stating that the case under discussion need not be followed, that, in short, the label *dictum* merely states a legal conclusion. Comment, Dictum Revisited, 4 Stan.L.Rev. 509 (1952).

That does not mean that the concept of *dictum* is illusory. A statement in an ordinary contracts case that the war in Vietnam was unconstitutional, all would agree, is *dictum*. Nor is the concept useless. Rather, the point is that because the force of precedent is an evolutionary process rather than a mere definition, the search for *dictum* in a case can easily mislead the reader. The concern of a lower court, for example, should be with implementation of what a higher court has to teach, rather than with a hostile use of labels in order to escape the binding effect of an unwanted "precedent." *Dicta* may be quite helpful in any search to understand the teachings of the higher court.

Although the word *dictum* is often used in an argumentative or derogatory sense, the label reminds us of some important lessons. In the first place, it serves as a useful reminder not to read too much into an opinion. A second function is to warn the reader that some statements in an opinion may be less carefully thought out than others, and that the weight to be given such portions of the opinion must be carefully considered. Finally, the concept of *dictum* reminds the reader that judicial power to make law derives from the need to decide actual cases. Judicial law-making is a tool to be used with great care. Widespread use of *dicta* increases the risk that that lesson of restraint will be forgotten, as the court tries to explain, for example, how a new rule will work in fact situations far removed from the case at bar. That restraining function of the *dictum* in a case serves as a natural limitation on the scope of the precedent; by terming the nonessential parts of a case *dictum,* a court refines the focus of the earlier case, thereby limiting its scope for future application.

§ 4.15 Determining the Scope: Extracting the Precedent

This section illustrates how a case can be "worked" in order to extract its holding. The reader is cautioned to remember, however, the previous discussion on scope of precedent.

The well-known case of Hadley v. Baxendale (1854), provides an easy example. There, a mill's crankshaft had broken. The miller took the shaft to a common carrier to be sent to another city to have a duplicate shaft made. Delivery of the new shaft was delayed due to "neglect" by the carrier, whereupon the miller sued the carrier for profits lost while the mill was shut down. The court, reversing a jury verdict for plaintiff, held that damages in a contract case must either "arise[e] naturally" from the breach, or be "such as may reasonably supposed to have been in the contemplation of both parties, at the time they made the contract, as the probable result of the breach of it."

That statement creates a legal rule, and is arguably necessary to the decision of the court (in order to resolve the issue of lost profits). Analysis of the scope of *Hadley,* therefore, can begin there. Is the stated rule too broad? Should its application be limited, for example, to cases involving common carriers, perhaps on the theory that because they must take all lawful carriage they should not be exposed to great liability for faulty performance? Although the case did involve a common carrier, there is little in the opinion to indicate the court was thinking in terms of carriers only; indeed, the court speaks of its rule applying to "any" breach of contract. Hence, the *Hadley* court itself, at least, viewed its rule as being of general application.

As a next step in analyzing the case, inquiry can be made concerning what it means to have dam-

ages "in contemplation"; that phrase could refer
simply to a reasonable expectation of the parties,
but it could also be read to require some form of
"tacit" agreement concerning special damages in
the event of breach.   Although language in the
opinion can be cited to support either reading, the
court seems to have had the latter possibility in
mind.   First, there is the decision itself, for the
court ruled that the jury should be instructed not
to award lost profits as damages, thus precluding it
from passing on whether plaintiff had reasonable
expectations concerning liability in the event of
breach.   Second, the court emphasized the failure
of the miller to inform the carrier that the plant
could not operate without the new shaft.   (The
unofficial statement of facts by the reporter suggests that such communication was made;   the
opinion, however, does not.)   That emphasis suggests, again, that the court was thinking in terms
of an actual understanding with respect to the
consequences of breach.   Third, the justification
for the contemplation rule—to permit the carrier
to self-insure by charging a higher fee—suggests
that the court was interested in communication of
information to the carrier that would have placed
it on notice of "special circumstances."

Extracting a precedent is a skill that requires a
good deal of practice, and a good bit of common
sense.   Facts, procedural setting, and the court's
explanation all help in that effort.   It must not be
forgotten, however, that the precedent cannot be
viewed in isolation, for its later history must also

be considered. *Hadley* itself is one example, for it took close to a century to resolve finally the definition of "contemplation of the parties." (In both America and England the "reasonableness" test prevailed.)

§ 4.16 Determining the Scope: Distinguishing the Precedent

The rule of *stare decisis* requires a court either to reach the same result in similar cases, or to overrule precedent. The key question, of course, is whether the cases are "similar". When a precedent bears some minimal resemblance to the case at bar a court might try to "distinguish" the two. Distinguishing the cases requires the court to explain why they should be decided differently. Since no two sets of facts are exactly alike, of course, all cases can be differentiated. Differentiation, however, does not *distinguish* until it is shown why the differences are legally significant. To make that showing requires, first, an isolation of the rule or principle established by the first decision; and, second, an analysis of why the different facts in the second case do not fit within that rule. That two-step analysis requires the court to determine the purposes behind the rule and then to decide whether those purposes would be furthered by the application of the rule to the case at bar. If they would not, then the cases can be fairly distinguished.

The use of Hadley v. Baxendale, discussed in the preceding section, as a precedent can illustrate this. Suppose in a later case involving the same basic facts, the mill hired an engineer to fix the broken mill shaft and explicit notice was given to the engineer that the mill would be shut down for as long as the shaft did not function. Assuming that the engineer breached by not performing the contract properly, would she be liable for consequential damages (lost profits)? It would not be hard to distinguish *Hadley* from the case supposed; that is, it would be relatively easy to find a principle that would be consistent with finding liability only in the engineer's situation, for hers is a much stronger case for finding the notification of "special circumstances" that *Hadley* deemed necessary before liability could be imposed.

Now suppose that the engineer had not been told of the consequences that would flow from breach. Could she be held liable for consequential damages, consistent with the rule in *Hadley?* Yes—if the required "contemplation" were read to mean "something a reasonable person in the shoes of the defendant would understand to be the natural and probable consequences of breach." Reading *Hadley* as establishing a test of reasonable foreseeability makes sense in terms of the policy mentioned in the opinion and arguably fits within the language of the opinion. Can it be squared with the result in the case, however? Possibly. To do so one would argue that the policy of risk allocation would not be furthered by informing a lowly clerk of a carrier as in *Hadley;* the clerk simply lacks ability and/or authority to handle the situation. The "reasonable" engineer, on the other hand, should be able to infer what will happen to the plant's profits if the shaft is not fixed in time. Cf. Armstrong v. Bangor Mill Supply Corp. (1929). Because the engineer should be able to make that inference, she can insure against the risk of liability for lost profits by charging the mill a higher price. Thus, the two situations could lead to different results; despite the apparent factual similarity, the difference could be reconciled.

The foregoing discussion of *Hadley* is not meant to exhaust that particular subject. That would take a long article itself. It is meant to suggest, however, the manner in which a precedent is approached to see if it is "on all fours" or if it is distinguishable.

§ 4.17 Redoing Precedent

As previously discussed, no decision exists in isolation and the lessons of any decision may have to be rethought in the light of experience. In retrospect the precedent may show an imperfect grasp of a principle. With the luxury of hindsight a later court may decide to restate the principle in order better to reflect the lessons learned from the precedent.

A classic illustration of this is MacPherson v. Buick Motor Co. (1916). There, a manufacturer sold a car to a retailer who resold it to the plaintiff. When a wheel fell off the car the injured plaintiff sued the manufacturer who defended on the ground that it owed a duty of care *only* to those who bought directly from it (in this case, the retailer).

The majority of the court, in an opinion written by Chief Judge Cardozo, held for the plaintiff. Cardozo concentrated his attention on a line of cases in which manufacturers and others were held liable to persons with whom they had not contracted. The first case he discussed, Thomas v. Winchester (1852), involved a mislabeled poison. Finding that the negligent labeling had put life in "imminent danger," the *Thomas* court permitted recovery. The defendant in *MacPherson* argued that an automobile was not "imminently" dangerous as is poison. Cardozo rejected that argument, basing his reasoning on cases that followed *Thomas*. In Statler v. George A. Ray Mfg. Co. (1909), for example, an exploding coffee urn led to the imposition of liability because the urn was "inherently" liable to cause damage if imperfectly constructed. From those and other cases Cardozo constructed a rule that did not rely on the "imminently" dangerous test: "But whatever the rule in Thomas v. Winchester may once have been, it has no longer that restricted meaning * * *. A large coffee urn * * * may have within itself, if negligently made, the potency of danger, yet no one thinks of it as an implement whose normal function is destruction." Then he stated a new rule: If an object is such that, negligently made, it is "reasonably certain" to cause personal injury, the manufacturer is "under a duty to make it carefully." The rule was qualified, however, by a limit suggested by a decision in which liability was not imposed. In Losee v. Clute (1873), the buyer, who had personally tested a steam boiler that later exploded, was not permitted to recover from the seller. Because of *Losee*, the rule laid down in *MacPherson*, therefore, required, for a duty to exist, in addition to "the element of danger," "knowledge that the thing will be used * * * without new tests."

Cardozo's opinion in *MacPherson* looked to case law for an understanding of how earlier courts had viewed the problem. Paying attention to what that look taught him, he devised a rule consistent with the earlier decisions, but one that used different language than that found in the earlier cases. By redoing the lessons of the past in new language, he was able to free the law in the area from the detailed analysis that had surrounded the imperfectly expressed rule of Thomas v. Winchester. Instead of focusing on the classification of something as "imminently" dangerous, the inquiry shifted to the reasonableness of expectations of manufacturer and consumer.

§ 4.18 Precedent and the Case of First Impression

The common law provides guidance even when the precedents are not really "on point," or even when there is apparently no law at all (what we call a case of "first impression"). The classic expression of this virtue came from Chief Justice Lemuel Shaw in the great case of Norway Plains Co. v. Boston & Me. R.R. (1854). It is a lengthy explanation, but well worth quoting in full.

> It is one of the great merits and advantages of the common law, that, instead of a series of detailed practical rules, established by positive provisions, and adapted to the precise circumstances of particular cases, which would become obsolete and fail, when the practice and course of business, to which they apply, should cease or change, the common law consists of a few broad and comprehensive principles founded on reason, natural justice, and enlightened public policy modified and adapted to the circumstances of all the particular cases which fall within it. These general principles of equity and policy are rendered precise, specific and adapted to practical use, by usage, which is the proof of their general fitness and common convenience, but still more by judicial exposition; so that, when * * * the general rule has been modified, limited and applied, according to particular cases, such judicial exposition * * * becomes itself a precedent, and forms a rule of law for future cases, under like circumstances.

Note well what Shaw says. The common law is composed of a "few broad and comprehensive principles." They are translated into practical effectiveness by "judicial exposition" in concrete cases. Because the common law is based on "broad principles," a new situation can be resolved by reference to those principles. Recognition of this method of common law adjudication is fundamental to an understanding of how our legal system responds to pressure for change.

A famous example of this process at work involves recognition of a cause of action for invasion of privacy. The modern genesis was a law review article, Warren and Brandeis, The Right to Privacy, 4 Harv.L.Rev. 193 (1890). The authors noted that the law did not recognize, as such, an action for damages to "feelings"; they believed, however, that existing case law did recognize "the principle * * * of an inviolate personality." Case law on privacy begins with Roberson v. Rochester Folding Box Co. (1902), in which plaintiff sought damages on that theory from a company that used, without permission, her likeness in its advertising. The majority declined to recognize the action. In doing so it examined a number of cases that Warren and Brandeis had cited in support of their position. The *Roberson* majority concluded that none of the cases discussed supported plaintiff's claim: "On the contrary, each decision was rested either upon * * * breach of trust or that plaintiff had a property right * * * which the court could protect."

Examination of a few of the cases discussed by the court shows how they could have been used to support plaintiff's claim, if the *Roberson* majority had been willing to reexamine the reasoning of the earlier decisions and extract from them a new principle. The first, Prince Albert v. Strange (1849), arose when the royal couple, after having made some family etchings, hired S to make copies for friends. S, however, made some copies for himself and sold them to the defendant. When defendant proposed to invite the public to see the etchings the Prince Consort sought an injunction. That request was granted, the Chancellor ruling that S had committed a breach of trust, and that the Prince had a "property interest" in the etchings.

The second case, Pollard v. Photographic Co. (1889), arose when a commercial photographer sold copies of a picture he had taken of the petitioner. The court granted an injunction on the ground that the photographer had breached an implied contract not to use the negative for any purpose other than to make prints for petitioner.

Gee v. Pritchard (1818), was also discussed in *Roberson*. As that court described the earlier case, "B attempted to print a private letter written him by A, and he was restrained on the ground that the property of that private letter remained in A, B having it only for the qualified purpose for which it was sent to him." Hence, the *Roberson* court viewed the *Pritchard* decision as based on the sender's continued property interest in the letter.

None of those three cases compelled a decision for the plaintiff in *Roberson*. If that court had examined each more closely, however, it might have found considerable support for her claim of privacy. Consider *Pritchard,* the last case, involving the letter. The court could have viewed the letter as a gift, and a completed gift (here by receipt) effectively transfers property. The decision, therefore, arguably ran counter to expectations derived from settled property law. The court, it could be supposed, departed from those expectations because it believed the sender had an interest that should be protected (an interest that we would label "privacy") insuring that his inner thoughts and feelings contained in the letter would not be made public. The *Pritchard* court, however, did not have available the concept of privacy and so it used the term "property interest." Had the *Roberson* court been alert (and receptive to a different outcome) it could have seen the policy the *Pritchard* court was groping for and reformulated the precedent in terms of protecting an interest in privacy.

A similar process could have occurred with respect to *Pollard.* There the court implied a contract not to use the negative of the portrait for other purposes. As every student of contracts knows, however, a contract (or, more properly, a clause in a contract) can always be implied; the interesting question is, *should* it be implied? Because contracts are implied to protect party expectations the question could have been rephrased: what were the parties' expectations in *Pollard* that led to the implication of a contract? The answer presumably would have been, when petitioner sat for her picture she had not expected that part of the benefit she was conferring on the photographer would be the right to sell her likeness to the public. Why not? Because unwanted distribution of her picture would injure her feelings; it would, in short, invade her "privacy."

The case involving Prince Albert and his etchings can also be reformulated. The court said that S had breached the trust placed in him. But to call something a "trust" is simply another way of labeling a legal obligation. What is the source of that obligation? There was clearly an expectation on the part of the royal family that the etchings would not be distributed without their consent. Again, that is another way of saying invasion of privacy. (This view is supported strongly by language in the Chancellor's opinion, for he mentioned that "privacy is the right invaded.")

Each of these cases, then, can be seen as based on a principle which would cover privacy. An alert court could have gone to them and extracted that principle. This can be shown schematically.

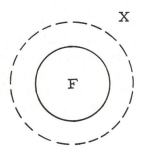

A case has a hard core of facts (here "F"), and a minimum decision—at the least each case says, on these facts, plaintiff (or defendant) wins. Each case, however, also carries possibilities for expansion of meaning into higher levels of generality ("X"—marked by a broken line to show the possibilities of expansion are not limited.) The case can be read more broadly as a "groping"—Dean Pound's word—for something else, a principle perhaps so unclear that it cannot yet be named. After a while a court can come along, view the cases with a fresh eye, and say *this* is what those cases really were trying to say. The technique of reformulation is as old as the common law. In the Fourth Institute (*circa* 1630), Sir Edward Coke, the greatest common lawyer of all, wrote: "Let us now peruse our ancient authors, for out of the old fields must come the new corn."

Reformulation can work in reverse; that is, a precedent may have to be narrowed. Another case discussed in *Roberson,* Schuyler v. Curtis (1895), illustrates this well. *Schuyler* was a suit to enjoin the erection of a statue of a dead woman, the suit brought by a relative of the decedent. The court denied relief. This precedent can be read to deny the existence of a right to privacy. Yet if the basis of that right is protection of "feelings," as suggested by Warren and Brandeis, then the potentially broad scope of *Schuyler* can be narrowed (from "X" towards "F") on the ground that the dead have no feelings (or at least none that the law should recognize). Whether the feelings of the living are worthy of protection is, of course, a question upon which *Schuyler* sheds little light.

§ 4.19 A Special Problem in Stare Decisis: Summary Disposition

The preceding sections have argued that in order to understand a precedent it is necessary to understand its reasoning. If no reasoning exists, the precedent is difficult to apply. A reminder of that problem involves the Supreme Court's efforts to explain to lower courts the precedential effect of either a summary affirmance or a dismissal for want of a substantial federal question. The problem arose because the Court, until quite recently, disposed of a large number of such cases within its mandatory jurisdiction on motion. Because those cases are within the Court's mandatory jurisdiction it would seem that the Court must either dispose of them on the merits or find jurisdiction lacking; hence, it can be argued that a decision on the merits by the Supreme Court binds lower courts within the same judicial hierarchy. It can also be argued, however, that an opinion disposing of a case with less than plenary consideration (that is, with less than full briefing, and without oral argument), and with a very short, conclusory opinion, has no precedential value; after all, the decision may not be based on adequate information, and there is no reasoning available to suggest the range of conduct that it controls. A number of lower courts have expressed this position. In Serrano v.

Priest (1971), for example, the California Supreme Court held that a summary disposition was similar in precedential effect to a denial of certiorari.

The Supreme Court has not opted for that position. In Hicks v. Miranda (1975), the Court held that its decisions on matters within its mandatory jurisdiction were binding on lower courts, at least to the extent that the issues in the earlier case and the one at bar were "sufficiently the same" so that the earlier case was a "controlling precedent." Unfortunately, *Hicks* did not explain precisely how lower courts were to determine the scope of the precedent established by a summary affirmance.

Several techniques are available to accomplish that task. It might be possible, for instance, to examine the scope of the opinion below (the one that was affirmed), but as Chief Justice Burger noted, in a summary affirmance, "we affirm the judgment but not necessarily the reasoning by which it was reached." Fusari v. Steinberg (1975) (Burger, C.J., concurring). That certainly is clear. The lower court might have found, for example, that a city ordinance did not violate the First Amendment; the Supreme Court might agree with the result, but still disagree substantially with the standard used below. The Supreme Court's agreement with lower court opinions should not be inferred from the Court's summary disposition, lest the technique be robbed of much of its labor-saving quality. If summary disposition were seen as precedent for the full scope of lower court opinions, the Supreme Court would be forced to consider the quality of the opinions below and could no longer pronounce judgment on the record.

Another technique to ascertain the scope of the precedent established by summary disposition was suggested in *Hicks:* examine the jurisdictional statement, the motion to affirm, and the replies filed by appellant. Unfortunately, this technique is also unsatisfactory. As Justice Brennan observed shortly after *Hicks,* the rules of the Court do not encourage "extended treatment of the merits" in those papers; rather, their purpose is "to apprise the Court of issues" that the parties believe will influence the Court's decision to grant plenary review. Colorado Springs Amusements, Ltd. v. Rizzo (1976) (Brennan, J., dissenting). It would be extremely difficult, therefore, to reconstruct the train of thought that led to the disposition solely by examing those documents. Moreover, those documents are not as readily available to the Court's consumers as are the Court's opinions.

Given such difficulties, it is not surprising that the application of *Hicks* created problems for lower courts. This can be illustrated by the case that explained *Hicks,* Mandel v. Bradley (1977) (*per curiam*). In *Mandel* the lower court had declared unconstitutional the filing requirements of Maryland's election law. The court below had based its decision on Tucker v. Salera (1976), in which the Supreme Court had summarily affirmed a lower court's invalidation of Pennsylvania's election filing procedures, requirements that were similar to, but by no means identical with, those contained in the Maryland statute. In *Mandel*, however, the Supreme Court injected a note of realism into the question of precedential value:

> Summary affirmances * * * without doubt reject the specific challenges presented in the statement of jurisdiction and do leave undisturbed the judgment appealed from. They do prevent lower courts from coming to opposite conclusions on the precise issues presented and necessarily decided by those actions. After *Salera*, for example, other courts were not free to conclude that the Pennsylvania provision invalidated was nevertheless constitutional.

As Justice Brennan's concurring opinion noted, the Court's emphasis on issues "necessarily decided" seems to require inquiry into whether the affirmance was based "even arguably upon some alternative constitutional ground." If not, then the summary disposition controls the resolution of similar issues in later cases. The difficulty comes in deciding when issues are "similar." Normally, that would be done by analogy, discussed in § 4.21. That task becomes quite difficult, however, in the absence of an opinion that shows what facts the Court believed to be important, a rule disposing of the case, and a justification for that rule—the factors that help us determine the scope of a precedent. To some extent, of course, it might be possible to reason by analogy from what was "necessarily" decided, but that task must be undertaken with care since the absence of expressed reasoning greatly limits the ability of others to know why the court affirmed. In short, summary disposition limits the scope of a decision, and hinders its extension to control related cases by analogy.

§ 4.20   Precedent and "Authority"

When precedent is used to justify a decision, it is called authority. Judges work with many forms of authority in analyzing the problems before them and in justifying the decision reached. Cases, treatises, statutes, the plays of Shakespeare, the works of Lewis Carroll, all comprise the raw material with which judges work their magic. Not all authority is created equal, however, and each must be individually evaluated if it is to be employed properly.

Controlling Authority. A decision by a higher court (or at least a majority thereof) in the same judicial system (see § 2.2) of course controls the disposition of any similar case. The lower court cannot question the validity of that precedent. Instead, the lower court should strive generously to understand the teachings of the precedent and implement it in the case at bar.

Occasionally, a lower court will ignore an apparently controlling precedent on the ground that it has been overruled *sub silentio*. By that the court means that later decisions by the high court have undermined the force of the precedent to such an extent that predictability and consistency in decision-making argue that it should *not* be followed. A court that reaches that conclusion must be very careful in so doing, for litigants and lawyers can still rely on a decision that has only been discredited and not formally interred.

Persuasive Authority. "Persuasive" authority comes from a source that is not controlling. A Kansas decision, of course, does not control a decision in Minnesota, but the reasoning and analysis of the Kansas decision may persuade the Minnesota court to reach the same result.

The term "persuasive" authority suggests that the important quality is the ability of the would-be authority to persuade. Hence, the depth of its research, the quality of its analysis, the sensitivity to the implications of the approach all must be considered by a court before it decides to follow the authority. This is a task that must be followed no matter what the source of the authority: be it decisional law, the Restatements, or the treatises of eminent scholars such as Prosser or Corbin. In every instance each court must determine for itself the wisdom and desirability of the course suggested. Finally, the court, if it uses authority to justify a decision, must explain in the opinion why it believes the authority is "authority." In short, it is not enough merely to "cite"; a court must also explain. That task seems inescapable for a court to satisfy its obligations of reasoned and consistent decision-making.

But there is more authority to a precedent than persuasiveness. Consider the Restatements. Whatever their merit, they are widely followed by many courts and by attorneys seeking to understand how a problem may be resolved. Because of that widespread use, a court, to some degree, is pushed by the need for uniformity in decision-making to adopting the solution offered by the Restatement. This push may not be very strong, but it is another factor to be considered in deciding how much weight to accord an authority. Put somewhat differently, authority is sometimes used or consulted, apart from its inherent persuasiveness, to insure that a decision fits within the mainstream of the law. Again, however, it is vital that a court explain why it believes it needs to follow a less desirable course of action.

The String Citation. One vice in the use of authority that besets both bench and bar is the citation to a "string" of authority, none of which is discussed by the author. Such usage fosters a belief that the author has not analyzed the authority referred to, but, instead, has merely taken a group of citations from a convenient reference. That, of course, is not an adequate substitute for a discussion of why the authorities cited are relevant (a reader of string cites sometimes wonders) and why the writer believes them to be important. At the very least, string cites should be followed by parentheticals which explain their relevance. Absent such a presentation, the reader of an opinion, for example, must wonder whether a court that has disposed of a problem with a string cite has indeed devoted some thought of its own to the problem.

Sometimes a string cite seems to be used to show how the decision accords with the great weight of authority. If that is the goal, however, the court should not pretend to have analyzed all cited authority; a reference to a source collecting those decisions would better reflect the use to which the court was putting the authority.

§ 4.21 Legal Reasoning

An appropriate way of ending a discussion on precedent is to discuss legal reasoning. The two are closely related. Many forms of reasoning can be used by a judge writing an opinion, ranging from formal logic to informal induction. Generally, an opinion is written in the form of a syllogism. In most cases there is little need to look beyond the syllogism, for the premises and conclusion leap readily to mind: "This case involves a defense based on inadequacy of consideration; courts do not question the adequacy of consideration, and, therefore, the defense will be rejected." Given scarce and expensive judicial resources, most cases, perhaps, merit no more visible effort. But there is a danger in syllogistic reasoning for it is seductive with the allure of apparent certainty, while an opinion that explains the manner in which judgment was exercised may be a good bit more difficult to write. The path of the syllogism, however, can lead to mechanical jurisprudence if it leads the judges to overlook two other vital forms of legal reasoning—the selection process exercised in the choice of legal rules and policies, and the use of reasoning by analogy in the application of precedent.

The process by which judges select rules and policies will be discussed in Part C of this Chapter. It is indispensable to the reasoned opinion.

Analogical reasoning proceeds by examining two (or more) patterns of facts to see if they are sufficiently similar to be embraced by the same legal rule. To take a simple example, Case A holds that a driver who crosses the center line of a highway has been negligent. In Case B, now before the court, the defendant driver crossed the center line to avoid a child who had darted out into the road from an adjoining street. Is Case B controlled by Case A? What is similar; what is different? Which is more significant? To set the problem up as a syllogism (that is, to use deductive reasoning) is useless. The important question in the case is *whether* the ordinary rule of negligence should be applied to conduct that saved the life of the third person. That question can only be answered by inquiry into the significant policies that the doctrine of negligence seeks to achieve and whether they would be furthered by holding the driver in B liable. In short, in order to answer whether Case B is controlled by Case A, the court must inquire into the reasons that led to the decision in A and whether B is similar enough to A for the reasons to apply in both. That is reasoning by analogy.

Suppose that the driver in B is held not liable. In a subsequent case, C, a driver had an accident when he crossed the center line, but this time the driver swerved to avoid a squirrel that had wandered onto the road. Is this case more like A or more like B? The only way a court can answer that question is to examine the policies served by the respective holdings in those cases, and then decide which would best be advanced by application in C. Ultimately, the judge must identify a policy and establish a rule that explains and reconciles all three decisions.

Because the values recognized in cases A and B cannot be quantified, the decision cannot be reduced to a formula. Because it cannot be reduced to a formula, the weight assigned to all of the factors—and even their relevance—depends on the judge's appreciation of each factor and his understanding of the goals of our society. Judging, therefore, requires selection and evaluation of values—*judgment,* in short—as well as reasoning.

PART C
JUDICIAL LAW MAKING

The preceding several sections discussed the sources judges can turn to when creating precedent. The sections that follow discuss issues related to that task: whether judges do make law, the arguments against judicial law-making, and the questions of judicial abstention and discretion.

§ 4.22　Do Judges Make Law?

This question has occupied the attention of many commentators on the common law. Thorough discussion of the issue can be quite difficult, for the answer depends in large part on the way in which the terms "make" and "law" are defined; that is, the question may turn on semantics. The problem, however, can be quickly outlined.

To Sir William Blackstone, writing two centuries ago, it was clear that judges did not make law; they merely announced it. A judge was "the living oracle of the law" (see § 2.3), and the basis for judicial pronouncements was the fully formed custom of the English people. An oracle, of course, can misread the entrails spread before him, but to Blackstone and other adherents of the "declaratory" theory of law (also discussed in § 4.29), a judge's opinion merely gave *evidence* of the law; it was not the "law" itself. Judges, in that sense, did not "make" law.

If we use the working definition of law earlier sketched out (§ 4.3), however, it becomes clear that judges do, indeed, make law. In fact, they *must* make law. That is a function of two commands, the necessity of deciding cases properly before them, and the rule of *stare decisis*. Judges, therefore, cannot escape law-making. To put this differently, each decision controls other cases. A command by a court is authoritative and forms the basis for action by other judges, by businesses, prosecutors, police officers, and all of the other persons in our society who must inform themselves of the likely reaction of the court to particular problems that may arise. Thus, judicial decisions are law; because judges constantly remold the clay used in the judicial process, sometimes reshaping it a little, sometimes a lot, even occasionally discarding a finished piece and making a completely new one, it seems accurate to say that they make law. The reader should also bear in mind, however, that for most judges the process is not one of free-wheeling creativity, but instead requires that close and careful contact be kept with the work of the other potters in the workshop, and the needs and desires of the public who consume their wares.

§ 4.23   The Creation of Precedent

The discussion of precedent thus far has skirted a difficult issue. What are the sources of the law? How is a precedent created? Without the guidance of prior decisions, how does a court *know* what is the best rule? Those problems are most acute where there is not case law on point (what we call the "case of first impression"), although they arise any time a court modifies precedent, or, indeed, whenever a court decides that an existing rule should be maintained.

A judge considering the adoption of a new rule must consider a number of factors. What ends will the proposed rule serve? How effectively will it achieve those ends? Why are those ends desirable? How well will it fit within the framework of existing rules? To answer those questions—or even to attempt to answer them—the judge must have a set of ultimate values to serve as a framework in which to fit the analysis of those questions. Examination of those values, such as the jurisprudential issues mentioned in § 4.2, is beyond the scope of this *Nutshell*. It is possible, however, to examine some of the sources that our judges draw upon in considering the adoption of a new rule.

The search will begin with case law and statute, seeking analogous, if not controlling, authority. Beyond that, all the learning of our culture can be employed in the search: philosophy, history, economics, psychology, custom, fundamental values. In short, almost all of human endeavor and thought provides grist for the judicial mill. The following sections illustrate how judges use those sources.

a. Case Law as a Source

The first place a judge will turn to for guidance is case law. We have already examined the process by which this works even in the case of first impression (§ 4.18). Let me give another example.

The common law judge has available for use a wealth of ideas and concepts in the case law that can be put to good use when the making of new law seems appropriate. Relying on well-established legal principle makes the court's break with the past less revolutionary (or at least appear to be so) for the opinion can show how the present decision rests firmly on those of the past. Continuity of doctrine also provides a base for understanding the scope and method by which new decisions will be applied. A famous example of this is Marvin v. Marvin (1976). In *Marvin* the court held that a woman who had cohabited with a man for six years could properly state a cause of action against him for a division of property accumulated in his name during that period. The *Marvin* decision achieved a good deal of publicity partly due to the personal fame of the defendant, an actor, but also because it was widely believed to reflect the values of a society in which less formal family relations were becoming both more common and more accepted. The legal analysis of the impact of those changing values was firmly grounded in common law concepts.

The complaint in *Marvin* was founded on express contract, a claim seldom recognized in this type of case due to the nature of the relationship. The California court, however, began its analysis of the problem by removing a barrier to the enforcement of such agreements when it decided that as long as that agreement was not made "in contemplation of sexual relations" it could be enforced. Once that barrier was removed, the court was free to apply a huge body of existing contract law to the problem. Similarly, the court's statement that implied-in-fact contracts between persons such as the litigants in *Marvin* would be enforced, tied cohabitant agreements into the mainstream of contract law.

The *Marvin* court went further, however, and the far-ranging importance of the decision rests as well on its recognition that express contracts of the sort alleged by the plaintiff in *Marvin* would not be common, nor would implied contracts, because party expectations, the heart of implied contract law, really do not exist in this area. The court, therefore, went on to suggest other available remedies, such as constructive trusts and *quantum meruit,* in order that the plaintiff may "assert her equitable interest in property acquired through her effort as does any other unmarried person." Once again, the court relied on remedies that were well-established, and although the specific application might be novel, analogy to existing use of the remedies would help their development in this area. Further, the court could count on commentary by other courts and by scholars to illustrate how the remedies mentioned could be applied to different fact situations likely to be litigated.

Building on prior law is a very important technique for judges; of course, that law does not answer all the questions presented in a case, but it does provide a frame of reference for analyzing problems as they arise. Although precedent can be quite useful in the development of the law, at times a court must frame an opinion that puts a problem into better perspective by rethinking the manner in which it should be approached. Justice Cardozo did precisely that in MacPherson v. Buick Motor Co. (§ 4.17), as did Justice Tobriner in the majority opinion in *Marvin,* where he recast the problem in the framework of fair dealing among unmarried couples: "Judicial barriers that may stand in the way of a policy based upon the fulfillment of the reasonable expectation of the parties to a nonmarital relationship should be removed." By that edict, Tobriner brought the contract rights of unmarried couples into the mainstream of the law.

b. Statutes as a Source of Law

A court exercising its law-making power may also turn to legislation for guidance. A constitutionally valid statute operates in its own sphere as law, for it controls all conduct coming within its ambit. A statute may in addition be viewed as a *source* to be used to show how a problem should be solved. Although the language of the statute does not expressly control the situation before the court, the policies the legislature sought to achieve in passing the law may help the court decide the case now before it. This section considers some ways in which that occurs.

i. Control by Implication. One common example of using a statute as a basis for judicial law-making involves the creation, in an action on a contract, of a defense based on the belief that the contract should not be enforced because it violates "public policy." To determine the content of that term courts will often look at statutory law in the area to see if denying enforcement to the contract at bar would further the policy embodied in those statutes. This is easy enough in the case of an illegal contract, a contract to murder being obviously unenforceable. To take a more likely example (at least one more likely to be seen inside a courtroom), a contract to violate the antitrust laws would also be unenforceable. Even when the contract itself is perfectly legal, if its procurement violated a statute it will be made unenforceable. An example is United States v. ACME Process Equip. Co. (1966), in which the Supreme Court held that violation of the Anti–Kickback Act (a federal criminal statute) would lead to invalidation of the contract involved.

A closely related problem involves the question of whether a court should imply a remedy when a statute has been violated even though there is no express statutory authorization for doing so. Although the problem may often be viewed, as many courts do, as one of statutory construction, it is both convenient to deal with the problem at this point and instructive as to the relation between legislative and judicial law-making.

A statute either prohibits activity or imposes duties. The only enforcement mechanism expressly provided in the text, however, might be the imposition of criminal penalties, or commitment of the problem to an administrative agency. Suit then is brought by someone aggrieved, claiming that although he is among the class protected by the act's prohibitions or requirements, it provides him no effective remedy for harm suffered. Should the court grant the request for relief?

That problem is one the common law has faced for centuries. A maxim—*ubi jus, ibi remedium* ("where there is a right there is a remedy")—was developed early on and suggests one solution. British courts even today routinely apply the maxim and imply remedies for private causes of action. American courts are generally more hesitant. In some areas, however, our courts have not been reluctant to grant a remedy not expressly provided by statute. The most familiar example is probably negligence *per se.* In those cases a court will find that a person who violated a statute (such as storing explosives improperly, or driving recklessly) has been negligent—without need to introduce further evidence on that issue. (The plaintiff, of course, must still establish causation, harm, etc.) In doing so courts have recognized that the statute has defined the standard of care required in those situations. Because the duty has been so defined there is little worry that imposition of liability will come as an unfair surprise to a defendant. Calling the violation negligence *per se* helps both to enhance the effect of the statute as a deterrent to wrongful conduct and to provide relief in tort for those who were to be protected by the law.

If, on the other hand, implication of a private remedy would not further the statutory purpose, relief may be denied. Failure to register an automobile properly, for example, has generally not led to the creation of implied tort remedies because the registration statute creates a duty that runs to the state and not to someone injured in a collision with the improperly registered automobile. Hence, the victim is not in the class the statute seeks to protect. And although a private remedy might help deter improper registration, most courts have believed that sanction too severe to invoke for something as trivial as improper registration. See R. Posner, The Law of Torts § 36 (4th ed. 1971).

The problem of when to imply a private remedy becomes more difficult when the legislature has created an administrative solution to the problem before it but has not expressly addressed the question of private remedies. In deciding whether to grant a private claim of right the courts have looked to a number of factors. Cannon v. University of Chicago (1979), discusses the Court's possible lines of analysis.

The petitioner in *Cannon* alleged that she had been denied admission to medical school because she was a woman. She sued the school under Title IX of the Education Amendments of 1972, 20 U.S. C.A. § 1681. The lower courts denied her relief on the ground that Title IX did not grant a private cause of action. In holding for petitioner the Supreme Court used a four-step inquiry to analyze the problem, which it viewed as one of "statutory construction."

(1) Was the statute "enacted for the benefit of a special class of which the plaintiff is a member"? The *Cannon* Court answered that question by focusing on whether the statute was designed to "benefit" persons discriminated against on the basis of sex, or, instead, to prohibit discrimination by educational institutions. The Court had no trouble in finding an intent to benefit plaintiff's class, for Title IX begins by stating "No person * * * shall * * * be subjected to discrimination * * *." In reaching that conclusion the Court noted that "the right- or duty-creating language of a statute has generally been the most accurate indicator of the propriety of implication of a cause of action." Once it is found that the statute confers a benefit it is easy to invoke the deterrent rationale for implying a remedy.

In contrast, the Supreme Court, shortly after *Cannon,* found no implied cause of action in § 17(a) of the Securities Exchange Act of 1934, 15 U.S.C.A. § 78q(a), which requires brokers to maintain various records. Because § 17(a) did not "prohibit certain conduct or create federal rights in favor of private parties," the Court would not imply a private cause of action from the statute. Touche Ross & Co. v. Redington (1979).

(2) Does the legislative history suggest any intent by Congress with regard to private causes of action? In National R.R. Passenger Corp. v. Na-

tional Ass'n of R.R. Passengers (1974), the Court
had focused on the absence of evidence that any
committee member believed private suits would be
possible under the Act, and concluded that such
silence indicated that the committee was not in
favor of private actions. In *Cannon,* however, the
Court found comfort in the fact that statutes similar to Title IX in wording and concept had been
found to imply remedies, and that Congress could
be presumed to have been aware of those decisions
when it passed Title IX.

That use of legislative history is dubious. Apart
from the fact that legislative silence is the most
unreliable form of legislative "history" (see § 5.21),
it is unlikely that a search for legislative intent on
this issue will yield anything of value. Quite simply, it is unlikely that Congress has *any* intent on
the existence of private remedies; it either has not
considered the issue at all, or it has not been able
to effect a consensus that it feels can be expressly
embodied in the proposal. Similarly, the presumption of legislative "awareness" and "acquiescence"
does not correspond to what in fact went on in that
body. Better would be a search in the history for
the answers to legislative goals, the next subject
discussed in *Cannon.* Still, the Court seems committed to rifling the legislative history for whatever comfort it can find therein.

(3) Will a private cause of action interfere with
the statutory goals? In Securities Investor Protection Corp. v. Barbour (1975), the Court had noted

that "public interests"—as well as those of private litigants—were implicated by the statutory scheme, and that an agency could consider third party interests better than could a court. Further, conflicting precedent on issues raised by third parties (in different districts or circuits) could render achievement of agency goals much more difficult. In addition, in Cort v. Ash (1975), the Court noted that Congress had created a corporate entity to solve a public problem. Private litigation, therefore, would be inconsistent with the new entity's pursuit of its public goals.

In *Cannon,* by contrast, the agency charged with administering the statute welcomed the private action. The Court also believed that administrative relief (elimination of federal funds) was too clumsy and drastic a remedy to carry out effectively the goals of Title IX. A private remedy, therefore, helped further statutory purpose. That analysis was similar to an earlier and much cited decision, J.I. Case Co. v. Borak (1964), which permitted private actions to enforce proxy rules promulgated by the Securities and Exchange Commission largely because that agency was believed to lack resources sufficient to permit it to enforce adequately its own rules.

(4) Finally, the Court asked if implying a federal remedy would be "inappropriate because the subject matter involves an area basically of concern to the States." That statement reflects a presumption against unnecessary federal intrusion into lo-

cal matters. In *Cannon* that inquiry presented no problem; protection against discrimination is an important federal interest.

Since *Cannon* the Court has on occasion been less receptive to claims that an implied cause of action should be recognized. An example is Thompson v. Thompson (1988), where the Court refused to imply a private federal cause of action under the Parental Kidnapping Prevention Act of 1980. The majority opinion noted, however, that the implied cause of action doctrine was still alive and that in considering whether a cause of action should be implied, the "intent of Congress remains the ultimate issue." That intent, the Court added, must be inferred from language, statutory structure, or some source for a private remedy to be implied. Justice Scalia, concurring, suggested that "we should get out of the business of implied private rights of action altogether." That statement echoes a similar statement made by Justice Powell in his dissenting opinion in *Cannon*. Nevertheless, the rest of the Court does not seem interested in "get[ting] out of the business" of implying a private action.

ii. Equity and Analogy. It is sometimes said that a statute has a "spirit" as well as a "letter," and that the person interpreting it should seek to carry out the former as well as the latter. One phrase expressing the concept of statutory spirit, "the equity of a statute" is very old. In *24b of his *Institutes* Lord Coke in the early seventeenth century explained the term as "a construction made by the Judges that cases out of the letter of a statute yet being within the * * * cause of the making thereof shall be within the same remedy that the statute provided * * *." Coke was willing to construe a statute broadly in order to achieve its purposes; his willingness to do so reflects an expansive view of the role of judges in statutory interpretation. At the same time, that view recognizes the primary role of the legislature in the establishment of policy. In short, following the Biblical injunction, the court should carry out the spirit of the law as well as the letter thereof.

In succeeding centuries judges lost sight of this role. Legislative intrusion into judicial affairs was viewed with hostility—the doctrine that statutes in derogation of the common law should be strictly construed is one example. (See § 5.18). In this century, however, critics have urged judges to recognize that the legislature is a very good source of principles that can be used by a court seeking to solve problems not directly addressed by a statute. A statute can be used, in other words, as a source of reasoning *by analogy,* much as a court uses case law to reason by analogy (see § 4.21). Because the legislature consists of democratically elected representatives, it would seem that its views on "policy", as evidenced by the laws it enacts, should be given careful consideration by a court. Moragne v. States Marine Lines, Inc. (1970), provides an example. In that case, the widow of a longshoreman who was killed off the Florida coast brought an action against the longshoreman's employer alleging unseaworthiness as the cause of death. Seaworthiness, the traditional standard of care in admiralty law, imposes a stricter duty of care than does a standard based on negligence. Unfortunately for the widow, Florida's wrongful death statute provided recovery only for negligence. Recovery based on unseaworthiness was available under federal law only if the longshoreman had been injured, or if the accident had occurred outside the three mile limit. In the latter case the Federal Death on the High Seas Act provided recovery. Hence, statutory law provided no relief based on an unseaworthiness standard. Further, the judicial rule, dating from 1886, was that there was no common law right to recover in Moragne's situation.

Despite those obstacles the Supreme Court granted relief. Justice Harlan's opinion first noted that Congress and the states had passed a number of statutes that "made it clear that there is no present public policy against allowing recovery for wrongful death." The widespread adoption in many jurisdictions of legislation providing for wrongful death recovery helped the Court to resolve the case. Justice Harlan explained:

> The legislature does not, of course, merely enact general policies. By the terms of a statute, it also indicates its conception of the sphere within which the policy is to have effect. In many cases the scope of a statute may reflect

nothing more than the dimensions of the particular problem that came to the attention of the legislature, inviting the conclusion that the legislative policy is equally applicable to other situations in which the mischief is identical. This conclusion is reinforced where there exists not one enactment but a course of legislation dealing with a series of situations, and where the generality of the underlying principle is attested by the legislation of other jurisdictions.

Using that policy, the Court went on to overrule its own previous holdings forbidding wrongful death recovery in admiralty. The Court, in other words, found a source of policy in the statutes, both federal and state, and used that policy, by analogy, to decide an issue expressly not covered by those statutes.

Moragne is a wise decision. A court should be willing to search for policy in statutes, to recognize that the elected representatives of the people should have much to say concerning what the goals of society are and how they can best be achieved. Although explicit reliance upon this type of reasoning—such as Justice Harlan's in *Moragne*—is rare, the method is familiar. A frequently used example involves the Married Women's Acts passed in the nineteenth century. Those Acts, limited to the creation of certain express rights in married women (the right to own property, for example), were recognized by courts as expressing a policy that the common law should recognize more widely; in the end, a wholesale recognition of women's rights resulted from their passage.

A caveat must be entered with respect to reasoning by analogy from a statute. The danger is that a court will not fully recognize the reasons why the legislature did not expressly provide for the problem at bar. There may well have been a purpose sought by the legislature that would be defeated by application in the case at bar. In *Moragne,* for example, the Congress could have felt it improper to interfere with state control of "local" waters, a policy reflected by making the Death on the High Seas Act applicable outside the three-mile limit. If so, it could be argued that the Court's opinion in *Moragne* partially frustrated that purpose of the Act. Justice Harlan rejected that argument in *Moragne* (on the ground that Congress believed an adequate remedy existed for such cases), but he was careful to subject it to thorough analysis.

Recognition of the question of whether statutory purposes would be frustrated by extension by analogy is crucial. Once that problem is recognized, however, the process of using a statute as a basis for analogical reasoning will help a court to see the solution to a number of difficult problems. Doing so can also help insure that judically created policy will be well grounded in societal goals identified by the representative branch of government.

c. Fundamental Values

A court does not render a decision in isolation. Each one becomes part of the tapestry constantly being woven by the judges. The opinions sometimes add new fabric to the piece, and sometimes they unravel existing parts of the tapestry and put the space freed to other uses. The point of that metaphor is to drive home the observation that an opinion cannot be considered in isolation. A judge must harmonize each decision with what has gone before.

The sturdiest threads in the tapestry represent values that are deeply held by our society. Sir Edward Coke wrote almost four centuries ago of the "maxims" of the common law, precepts that represented "common right and reason" and that in his hands were elevated to a kind of quasi-constitutional status. Most famous is Coke's own decision in Dr. Bonham's Case (1610), where the maxim "No man shall be a judge in his own cause," played a key role. That maxim finds current usage in our own judicial decision making; see, e.g., Tumey v. Ohio (1926) (judge may not be paid from fines collected from defendants).

Fundamental values play an important role in judicial decision-making because they cannot be lightly transgressed by a court. An example is the notion of unjust enrichment, which can be traced back to Roman times, and later was the vehicle for the development of the law of quasi-contract. Unjust enrichment was used by the California Supreme Court to suggest a method of protecting unmarried cohabitants in the case of Marvin v. Marvin (discussed earlier in this section).

As Justice Holmes stated in Lochner v. New York (1905), "general propositions do not decide concrete cases," and a case like *Dr. Bonham's* where that does happen is an exception. Moreover, blind reliance on fundamental principles can be just another form of decision by pigeonhole (see § 4.7), where citation is substituted for analysis. Still, reference to fundamental values provides an indispensable touchstone for the court, helping it to maintain contact with those ideas society holds most dear.

d. Custom

Custom provides a basis for legal decisions. A court gives effect to custom because a particular practice shows what the expectations of a group were with respect to an issue. Custom, therefore, serves to provide a factual basis for decisions. It can also be a source of law itself.

English courts have long given effect to custom. In English practice a local custom could override the common law (the "custom" of the nation). According to Blackstone several criteria had to be met before that could happen: the custom had to exist continuously from time immemorial, and had to be reasonable, certain, and accepted as compul-

sory. (To exist from "time immemorial" meant
that the practice could not be shown not to have
existed in 1189 when Richard I became King.)

In this country a local custom could not of course
be traced back to 1189. American courts, therefore, have generally demanded only that a custom
be of long and general usage before it be given
effect. There are a number of different ways in
which that can happen.

i. Custom and Expectation. Perhaps the best
illustrations can be found in contract cases, especially those involving assertions of a meaning different than that normally attached to a word or
phrase. If both parties belong to a trade which has
a well-established trade usage—an internal dictionary as it were—the court will interpret language
in accordance with that usage. The following ex-
cerpt from Hurst v. W.J. Lake & Co. (1932), gives
some feeling for that process:

> [I]n the bricklaying trade a contract which fixes
> the bricklayer's compensation at "$5.25 a thou-
> sand" does not contemplate that he need lay
> actually 1,000 bricks in order to earn $5.25, but
> that he should build a wall of a certain size. In
> the lumber industry a contract requiring the
> delivery of 4,000 shingles will be fulfilled by the
> delivery of only 2,500 when it appears that by
> trade custom two packs of a certain size are
> regarded as 1,000 shingles, and that hence the
> delivery of eight packs fulfills the contract, even
> though they contain only 2,500 shingles by actu-

al count. And, where the custom of a locality considers 100 dozen as constituting a thousand, one who has 19,200 rabbits upon a warren under an agreement for their sale at the price of 60 pounds for each thousand rabbits will be paid for only 16,000 rabbits. (Citations omitted)

Custom, however, has a much larger role in contract than that of a mere dictionary. Contracts cannot provide expressly for all contingencies. What then happens when an unprovided-for event occurs? A contract is law privately made; agreements are enforced because the law deems it wise to protect the expectations of the parties within the limits set by "public policy." If the express terms do not provide an answer, a court will see if one can be supplied by inquiry into the expectations of the parties. The first place to look is private custom, the course of performance—past and present—between the parties: "[W]here the interpretation of a contract is fairly debatable, the court will adopt the practical construction which the parties to the contract have heretofore adopted, whether by conduct or otherwise." Fort Dodge Co-op. Dairy Marketing Ass'n v. Ainsworth (1933). If private custom does not help, the court will complete the contract, if possible, by referring to more general understanding concerning what parties can expect when they enter into an agreement. That is the basis, for example, of much of the law of mistake, a doctrine predicated in part on the assumption by the parties that something is or is not true. If the parties did not expressly allocate the risk that their assumption was not true a court will look to such factors as custom and surrounding circumstances to determine upon whom the loss must fall. (Often, even those indicia provide little help and the court's decision may be on the order of a coin flip; after the decision, however, future party expectations will be based on that decision.)

Much of commercial law developed as judicial ratification of custom. Over the years courts have ratified many new business devices designed to facilitate commerce (examples are the deed of trust and the reasonably prudent investor rule for a trustee). In adopting custom into law, the courts have been careful to inquire into the ubiquity of the custom. Courts also seem to feel more confident when ratifying a custom if it can be shown to have a sound business justification. When that is found, though, they are willing to go a long way.

Statutes sometimes recognize the desirability of giving effect to custom. The best example is the collective bargaining agreement entered into under the aegis of the National Labor Relations Act. As Justice Douglas noted in United Steelworkers of America v. Warrior & Gulf Navigation Co. (1960), "An agreement is more than a contract; it is a generalized code to govern a myriad of cases which the draftsmen cannot wholly anticipate * * *. It calls into being a new common law—the common law of a particular industry or of a particular plant." By recognizing the existence of this "new common law" an arbitrator is giving life not only to the local custom of a particular industry, but is also implementing a national policy.

At some point, of course, custom crystallizes into law. As the court remarked in Atkinson v. Brooks (1854),

> [U]ntil such rules become measurably settled by practice, they have to be treated as matters of fact, to be passed upon by juries; and when the rule acquires the quality of uniformity and the character of general acceptance, it is then regarded as matter of law. It is thus that most of the commercial law has from time to time grown up.

That hardening of custom into law is inevitable given the demand of uniformity and predictability. The issue then is taken away from the jury and left to the judge; custom has served its purpose of protecting party expectation.

ii. Custom and Duty. Tort law today places great emphasis on the role of custom in defining an individual's duties toward others. (Contract law also involves a definition of duties, but there the duties are reciprocal and consensual.) Negligent behavior is behavior that a reasonable person would not engage in; hence, the general duty of care in tort law is based on customary action. And, of course, the jury, the hypothetical great composite of reasonableness, determines whether that standard has been satisfied.

iii. Custom as a Limit on Duty. The more interesting problem in tort law concerns whether someone who conforms with customary behavior can escape liability for the consequences of that behavior. The leading judicial decision on this question is The T.J. Hooper (1932). That case involved a charge that a tug towing barges that foundered in a storm was unseaworthy. The basis of that allegation was the failure of the tug to have a radio that would have picked up warning of the storm's approach. At that time the coastal trade had not generally adopted the use of radios on board tugs.

The tug owner claimed that the general practice set "the standard of proper diligence." Judge Learned Hand responded:

Indeed in most cases reasonable prudence is in fact common prudence; but strictly it is never its measure; a whole calling may have unduly lagged in the adoption of new and available devices. It may never set its own tests, however persuasive be its usages. Courts must in the end say what is required; there are precautions so imperative that even their universal disregard will not excuse their omission.

He then noted that the practice in the trade was, in any event, not uniform and went on to reject the argument that custom should be viewed as the maximum standard of due care.

Surely Judge Hand was correct. Custom helps the court keep in touch with our dynamic society, but our society also has interests that may not be adequately protected in the development of the custom. The applicable standard, therefore, is due care, not common usage, for the law seeks to protect those who are affected by the actions of others and who may not have participated in the establishment of the custom. In *The T.J. Hooper,* for example, the failure of the tug owners to purchase radios did not result from a decision made in conjunction with possible adverse interests such as shippers and sailors. The decision was not, therefore, a bargained-for allocation of risk. In the absence of contractual efforts to avoid liability (to set privately the standard of care through allocation of risk among the contracting parties), the court must determine the adequacy of the efforts to maintain due care.

To give another example, suppose all ski resorts marked trails with pointed maple saplings and a skier who had been impaled by such a marker sued the resort, alleging that it should have used bamboo poles which would splinter and not cause injury. Should the industry practice absolve the owner from liability? In Marietta v. Cliffs Ridge, Inc. (1969), the answer was no. Society is interested in the protection of skiers and custom is merely one circumstance to consider when doing so. That decision reflects the statement of another court that "[i]n the long run usage must conform to reason." MacDougall v. Pennsylvania Power & Light Co. (1933).

iv. Custom and Judicial Creativity. Some writers have assigned custom a dominant or even exclusive role in judicial decision-making. That view is associated with the Historical School of Jurisprudence that flourished in the last century (see § 4.2), a school led in this country by James Carter. Carter believed that the role of the court was limited to giving effect to custom, and that only the legislature could "lead" society down new paths.

That view resembles the Blackstone "discovery" view of the law (see § 4.29) because the law is always "out there," and the judge's job is to try as best he can to "find" it. Carter's theory differs from Blackstone's, however, because custom is dynamic; thus Carter's system provided for change in a way that Blackstone's did not. In a sense, Carter's system is tautological: Judges, as products of their society, will adopt policies reflective of it, although judges, as well as law professors, can march to different drummers and adopt aberrational policies. That does not necessarily indicate agreement with Carter. A common law judge's creativity lies in drawing policy from a number of different sources and casting ideas suggested by patterns of behavior and social philosophy (see the discussion of the right of privacy in § 4.18). Such happenings originate in the society the judge reflects, but they also occur on paths different from those trod well enough to label "custom." It would be a mistake not to recognize this creative component of the judge's craft.

e. History

"A page of history," Holmes told us, "is worth a
volume of logic." New York Trust Co. v. Eisner
(1921). Without an appreciation of the historical
setting of the establishment and development of
legal rules and institutions it is difficult to understand fully the purposes they serve. Judges appreciate this need, for opinions often exhibit a good
deal of effort spent on establishing the historical
framework of a particular legal problem. A legal
system based on precedent (based, that is, on what
has been decided in the past or, in other words, on
history) simply cannot function unless the courts
work hard to place each decision—and each line of
decisions—in historical perspective.

Without resort to historical materials much of
our legal learning would be useless. As Benjamin
Cardozo reminded us in The Nature of the Judicial
Process 54 (1921), our law of real property, based
ultimately on feudalism, could not possibly be com-
prehended without help from history. So too with
the doctrine of consideration in contract law.

History also gives a sense of the weight of precedent. In Southern Pac. Co. v. Jensen (1917), Justice Holmes captured this when he wrote, "A common law judge could not say I think the doctrine of
consideration a bit of historical nonsense and shall
not enforce it in my court." Ancient doctrines
cannot be lightly cast aside. The pull of consistency and expectation are hard to resist. History's

hand, however, need not completely stay change. Holmes' example can be ours. Courts have over the past several decades nibbled away at the doctrine of consideration by developing concepts such as third party beneficiary and promissory estoppel (although those too have roots in the past). Consideration is by no means dead today, but it is somewhat frayed at the edges.

History, in short, has a lesson to tell, but each generation must determine that lesson for itself. One way that is done is by judicial interpretation of those lessons in the lawmaking process.

f. Other Sources

Courts may also turn to more specialized information in order to inform themselves properly before making a decision. Frequently consulted are psychology, economics and philosophy.

Psychology. Judges often borrow from psychology in the search for solutions to particular problems. In criminal law, for example, judges had to decide what test to apply to a defendant's claim that he was insane at the time the crime was committed. The Court of Appeals for the District of Columbia, in Durham v. United States (1954), the best known American case on the issue, rejected the "knowledge of right-wrong" test of responsibility for criminal behavior, replacing it with one that focused on whether the unlawful act was "the product of mental disease or defect." In doing so, the court drew heavily on the thinking of psychologists on the problem of criminal insanity. Two decades later the same court determined that the reliance on expert testimony fostered by *Durham* was interfering with the jury's exercise of its proper role and replaced *Durham* with a new test. United States v. Brawner (1972). *Brawner* also emphasized, however, the need for the law of insanity to reflect modern medical and psychological thought on the problem.

The civil law must also define insanity. A defense on a contract claim, for example, might be that the defendant should be discharged due to his mental condition at the time the agreement was entered into. That defense has long been recognized, and courts, in defining its limits, have drawn on the learning of psychologists. A leading case is Ortelere v. Teachers' Retirement Bd. (1969), where the court moved from a "cognitive" test (one that asks whether the defendant appreciated the consequences of her actions) to one focusing on the "mental illness" or "defect" of the defendant. The court predicated its holding on its understanding of modern "psychiatric knowledge."

Economics. Obviously, a judicial decision can have a significant economic impact. Today, sophisticated judges recognize the need to analyze the effect of their decisions upon the business life of the community. They have been aided in that effort by a substantial body of works by commentators on economics and the law.

The use of economic tools is most striking, of course, in antitrust law. Although antitrust law is grounded in statutes, courts have interpreted those statutes in open-ended fashion, often examining economic theory to help them understand the proper course to take. Today's interpretation of antitrust law displays a fondness for the tools of price theory (micro-economics) to solve problems that surely would have astonished the draftsmen of the Sherman Act. In United States v. E.I. duPont de Nemours & Co. (1956), for example, the Supreme Court inquired into the "cross-elasticity of demand" for cellophane to help it determine whether the defendant had monopoly power over the product it was charged with monopolizing.

Economic analysis has played an important role in other areas, such as tort and contract law. Tort law in recent years has shown an appreciation of the economic concept of external costs (an external cost is simply a cost associated with any activity that burdens someone other than the actor). The cases reveal that judges, worried about the phenomenon, have sought rules that would internalize costs. Hence, one reason for the development of strict product liability was to insure that the manufacturer of an airplane, for example, compensated all those who might be harmed in the normal course of operating the plane. In turn, the manufacturer would charge buyers enough to cover that risk. Nuisance law and the development of implied warranties of habitability in landlord/tenant law also reflect, in part, the perceived need to internalize costs.

Economic analysis also has an important role in contract law. In mistake cases, for example, courts inquire into risk allocation, an inquiry often centered on business expectations. Much of the law of unconscionability centers on business justifications for various commercial practices. Sometimes the analysis can become quite detailed, especially in damage cases. An example is Vitex Mfg. Corp. v. Caribtex Corp. (1967), where the court, asked by plaintiff to award overhead costs as part of its damages, analyzed in detail the difference between fixed and variable costs.

Philosophy and Moral Values. A judge represents the mixture of values of her culture. Set apart from society by specialized training as well as by individual characteristics, the "oracle of the law" (to use Blackstone's phrase, see § 2.3), still speaks for it. Her sense of what is fair and proper will reflect, albeit imperfectly, that of society. A sense of ethics and moral values is an important source of law making. It is also one whose content can change over time, a change that courts must be alert to perceive.

Consider the role of "freedom of contract" in decision making. In 1875 an English judge, Sir George Jessel, wrote,

> [I]f there is one thing which more than another public policy requires, it is that men of full age and competent understanding shall have the

utmost liberty of contracting, and that their contracts entered into freely and voluntarily shall be held sacred and shall be enforced by Courts of Justice.

Printing and Numerical Registering Co. v. Sampson (1875). In 1875 the philosophy of society, or at least of its dominant strata, was overwhelmingly in favor of full freedom of contract. Today, however, it is inconceivable that a judge could write that paragraph. Although our economy is still primarily *laissez-faire,* we have come to believe, for better or worse, that far more protection should be extended to the unwary consumer than was envisioned by Jessel. Duress, promissory estoppel, unconscionability, and implied warranty, are all doctrines that, despite roots in the past, have flowered in recent years to protect persons who exercise their "freedom to contract."

The weakening of an unrestricted *laissez-faire* philosophy has affected other areas as well. The demise of the fellow-servant rule provides another example. Well-entrenched in American jurisprudence by the end of the nineteenth century, the rule that a worker could not sue his employer for damages caused by the negligence of a fellow employee, could be defended by Justice Lemuel Shaw on the ground that the worker assumed that risk in the bargaining for his wage; in other words, his salary should bear a premium reflecting the risk associated with the job. Farwell v. Boston & Worcester R.R. Corp. (1842). Today, however, the fellow-servant rule is totally discredited. We believe that a worker generally lacks the power to bargain with respect to that risk, and may also be unaware of the degree of risk involved in his employment. Again, the change in society's attitude towards "freedom of contract" (and also toward workers) led to a significant change in the law.

g. Law and Fact

A difficult issue in legal decision-making involves the allocation of responsibility between judge and jury. The basic rule is easy to state. "Questions of law" are for the judge and "questions of fact" are for the jury. Lurking behind that simple statement lies a difficult question: How does a judge tell a "fact" question from a "law" question?

Sometimes it is easy to tell. There are pure *fact* questions—how fast was the defendant driving, or did the seller really say there were no termites in the house; these are questions that ask "what happened"—in other words, what are the historical facts? Then, there are pure *law* questions—does the First Amendment apply to defamation actions, or is an acceptance effective when mailed? These questions ask what legal rules control the case.

Sometimes, however, it is not so easy to tell the difference between the two categories. Consider a defendant sued for a defective design in a products liability action. The jury could be asked to return a general verdict ("Is the defendant liable?"), or its range of decision-making could be limited by instructions ("There can be no liability for a design defect unless the state of the art was such that the defendant should have recognized the problem and avoided it with its design.") The problem here is determining who gets to decide the question of *law application* (sometimes called a "mixed question of law and fact"). Does the jury, after being told by the judge the basic legal rules, apply that law to the facts it finds? Or does the judge apply the law to the facts that the jury finds? In other words, one way to distinguish between questions of law and fact is to ask how much control the court did (or should) exercise over the jury's decision-making. That control is exercised by treating the issue as one of law and then by giving the jury instructions which limit its ability to decide the case as it wishes.

A court which treats a problem as legal rather than factual, in other words, has laid down law. The legal statement contained in the jury instruction (or in the opinion which takes the case away from the jury by summary judgment, directed verdict, and related techniques) can be used to guide future action (by product designers, for example) and to control future courts. The judge trying to decide, therefore, whether an issue is one of law or fact should consider whether she wishes to control future behavior by establishing law. In doing so, she will address a number of questions.

First she will ask whether the facts are common and recurrent; if they are, then there is more need to make clear the rules of the game so that every one can try to follow them. That will also make decisions more consistent as well as enhance predictability.

Next she will ask whether the question is one that the jury can understand as well as the judge; it is much easier to ask the jury to determine whether a defendant was driving negligently than to ask whether it was designing products negligently. As the Supreme Court wrote a century ago: "It is assumed that twelve men know more of the common affairs of life than does one man, that they can draw wiser and safe conclusions from admitted facts thus occurring than can a single judge." Sioux City and Pac. R. Co. v. Stout (1873). In contrast, a judge is more likely to understand contract interpretation so that is usually a task reserved for the court.

The judge will also ask herself whether the issue is one that might lead the jury to show undue prejudice to one side. An example is § 2–302 of the U.C.C. which makes unconscionability a question for the court to decide.

Finally, the judge must decide whether an issue should be preserved for appellate review. It is much easier for an appellate court to review an issue if the jury's discretion has been limited by a special instruction after the question has been treated as a legal one; in contrast, if the issue has been part of a general verdict, the appellate court can only decide whether there was sufficient evi-

dence to permit a reasonable jury to find as it did.
The appellate court, in other words, can only review questions of fact under the clearly erroneous
standard.   On the other hand, the appellate court
can review questions of law without deferring to
the judgment below.   For that reason, appellate
review is much less effective for problems that are
treated as questions of fact.

h.   Burdens and Persuasions

A variation on the law/fact problem involves the
burdens of production and persuasion.   The party
with the burden of production (the plaintiff in an
automobile accident case, for example), must produce enough proof of the defendant's negligence so
that a reasonable jury could find for the plaintiff;
if the plaintiff does not satisfy that burden he has
failed—as a matter of law—to carry his burden,
and the case will never reach the jury.   No reasonable jury, in other words, could find for the plaintiff.

Once the plaintiff satisfies his burden of production, on the other hand, the defendant must produce evidence of a defense (evidence showing that
she was not negligent, for example).   If she does
not, then the plaintiff will have summary judgment entered in his favor;   if the defendant does
produce such evidence then the case will go to the
jury and it will decide the negligence question.   If
the defendant produces the right kind of evidence
(perhaps of contributory negligence), the burden of

production might shift back to the plaintiff and he must produce evidence showing that he was not contributorily negligent.

§ 4.24   Limits on Judicial Law Making

Judges make law in order to decide cases. They make as little or as much as is necessary to dispose of the case before them and give guidance for the future disposition of similar disputes. Because few effective formal restraints on their exercise of power exist, it might be thought that judicial lawmaking would be a freewheeling exercise. In practice, however, courts generally view the scope of their ability to make law somewhat differently. A number of factors contribute to judicial restraint in lawmaking even though judges (especially appellate judges) are not responsible in any real way to the electorate; their ability to give guidance is limited by both the issues that are brought before them and by the traditional style of the judicial opinion. Those limits are discussed in more detail below.

a.   *The Democratic Argument*

In theory, a legislator represents the will of the people. If his decisions are not correct he can be recalled at the polls. This is not true of a judge who decides a case incorrectly. Her decisions are effectively beyond the voice of the people, for although a decision can be overridden by the legislature, legislatures rarely take such action. Because the judiciary is not generally answerable to the voters, many believe that judges should be quite cautious when making new law.

There is merit to that argument; on the other hand, it would seem that a judge could err on the side of caution as easily as on the side of change. It may be that the argument based on democracy amounts to nothing more than an admonition that judges should look carefully before leaping. That look, however, might reveal to the court that the consequences of its decision cannot be fully predicted, and that extreme care must be exercised when it adjudicates in an area normally thought to be legislative.

Other factors limit the impact of argument based on democracy. Judges do not have complete freedom to do as they wish. The rule of *stare decisis,* the need to explain and justify decisions, to act with consistency and fairness, all help to keep judges generally from acting in too precipitous a fashion. To some, the restraints imposed by the judge's craft may seem flimsy, but they are, in fact, very real, for the judge has been trained since law school in their use; bonds not seen may still be felt. Another restraint on appellate courts comes from the fact that they are composed of several judges. A change can only be made by a majority, a factor that reduces the chance of too quick a change.

Finally, judges lack generally the potency to change deeply held societal beliefs. Segregated schools, for example, were declared unconstitutional in 1954, but effective relief did not come about until the passage of civil rights legislation a decade later. There are fundamental limits to the court's ability to change society. As usual, Justice Holmes captured this best: "I recognize without hesitation that judges do and must legislate, but they can do so only interstitially; they are confined from molar to molecular motions." Southern Pacific Co. v. Jensen (1917) (dissenting).

There is another facet of the democracy argument. Judges draw power not from the people directly but from the moral authority of their position as judges, and from the persuasiveness of the opinions they render. Such power is necessarily fragile; as a result it has been urged that the judiciary's capital stock of authority be carefully husbanded so that it not be depleted. That view is a helpful reminder; if taken too far, however, it can prove paralyzing. Of what good is the power we give judges unless they use it? The important role of the judiciary in our society cannot be filled adequately if judges hesitate to act because they fear a decision could affect their power adversely. Indeed, to a large extent we have tried to insulate our judges from just this worry by removing them from the electoral process. That removal, in addition, is an attempt to insure that judges decide cases without fear of personal consequences. A guess could also be hazarded that more power may accrue to a court when it acts from a sense of justice, rather than from fear.

b. Control Over Issues

To make law a court depends on the cases brought before it. The necessity of relying on the happenstance of litigation necessarily makes any attempt to create law in a systematic and sustained fashion very difficult. Further, the court depends to a large extent on the manner in which the parties frame facts and issues. A court concerned about the substantive law of defamation may find that neither party wishes to advance arguments in that area, each preferring to argue instead that victory should be his under the existing standard. It is also difficult, though not impossible, to recast the focus of a case at the highest appellate level. Inability to do so limits that court's power to place the case in a posture ideal for deciding an issue. Finally, the court depends on the parties for the presentation of data that will help inform it of the consequences of a particular course of action, data that bear on such questions as what is the custom of business in an area, or to what extent the insurance industry has relied on past decisions in the area of strict product liability. Counsel and court are engaged in a colloquy; if the former cannot supply the latter with the information that it needs, the quality of the law created from that colloquy will suffer.

Compare the legislative process to that outlined above. The legislature is free to examine any issues it chooses and can frame those issues in any manner that seems desirable. A full range of information can be provided both by a hearing and by evaluation by theoretically disinterested committee staffers. In those respects, therefore, the legislative process is more efficient for the making of certain kinds of significant law than the judicial.

But the judicial model cannot be compared fairly with an idealized version of what the legislature does. Legislators as well as courts face time pressures. Issues are often thrust on them by events, and outside forces such as the clamor of free-spending interest groups can also limit the way the issues are framed for resolution. The hearing process works well in theory, but in practice it is often a stylized presentation that has no impact on outcome. Disinterested staff may be hard to come by. Further, some state legislatures are virtually without committee staff, and thus are completely closed off from that source of assistance.

Nor is the "worst case" presentation of judicial ability to control the lawmaking process necessarily accurate. Litigation that calls for new law is generated by a changing society, one where existing rules chafe the economic and social order. It would be expected that pressure to clarify the law with respect to such problems would converge on the courts from a number of cases at more or less the same time. (Recent examples were provided by the need to clarify the law of commercial impracticability in the light of double digit inflation and rapid increases in the price of petroleum.) To be sure, those cases might not all arise within the same judicial system, but our nationwide system of precedent enables courts to refine solutions to problems by drawing on those attempted by other courts. Nor is a court altogether helpless if it believes counsel in a case will not be competent to provide it with the arguments and information indispensable to understanding what course of action to take. A court with discretionary jurisdiction might simply refuse to hear the case; another court could ask for briefs *amici curiae,* or perhaps appoint special counsel. To assist in that task, and in evaluating the presented data and arguments, a court can draw on significant outside resources. Few issues reach the appellate level without some consideration in scholarly and practical journals. In addition, an appellate judge generally has available one or more law clerks to assist in those tasks.

c. Limits of the Judicial Method

A legislature has a wide range of options available to it when it deals with a problem. In addition to ignoring the problem (an option not always available to a court (see § 3.11)), it can pass either a general statute or a very specific one; it can establish administrative agencies to propose and supervise a solution; in short, it can choose from among a multitude of flexible remedies.

A court does not have all of those options. Apart from some tinkering with special masters, courts have not turned to anything resembling an agency solution. The law of remedies has made vast strides in the past two decades (especially under the spur of school desegregation and other civil rights litigation), but judicial choices in this area remain limited; it would be a rare court, for example, that would award treble damages to a winning plaintiff without statutory authority in the manner of the Sherman Act.

Judges typically do not issue opinions that have the specificity of many legislative solutions. The conventional style of an opinion is geared to the facts of the case along with the elaboration of a few principles, and opinions are not treated as stating rules firmly embedded in concrete. Judges generally do not tend to issue opinions with the detail of, say, the elaborate system of priority of liens found in § 9–312 of the Uniform Commercial Code. A system of priorities can, of course, be extracted from cases in the area; analogous to § 9–312 were the cases establishing priorities among successive assignees of the same assignor. It can be done, but the process of extraction lacks the efficiency of the legislative fiat. In any event, courts do not make much use of definite "rules"; a statute might say that an action must be filed within one year from the date of the accident, but a court would say the action must be brought within a reasonable time ("laches"). Judge-made law that establishes a concrete "rule" is unusual enough to excite comment among normally unflappable students. Even when an example can be found the specificity of a court-made rule is usually a short-hand way of expressing a more general goal. The Rule Against Perpetuities, for example, which, very generally, prohibits tying up property for more than a "life in being plus 21 years," adopted 21 years as part of the permissible measure simply because that is (or was) the age of majority. Occasionally, examples can be found in which courts do use specificity in the decision to control closely future behavior. This is particularly true in the area of criminal procedure where courts believe precise guidance of police activity to be important. (Today, such guidance is often given through judicial promulgation of rules, a quasi-legislative process independent of litigation.) And, of course, injunctive relief can be very specific. Such orders, however, do not serve formally as precedent for future action. They are merely one judge's view of what constitutes a proper remedy to satisfy the needs of a particular situation.

There may be no satisfactory explanation for the judiciary's reluctance to go into such detail. Part of the explanation is historical, because the expectations of bench and bar based on historical roles as to the wisdom of judges acting creatively play a major part in constraining judicial freedom. The major functional reason for reluctance to go into elaborate detail centers on the need to be able to reshape precedent as necessary, a task that general language makes easier. A price must be paid for generality, however, in the loss of certainty. That loss must be considered as a court goes about its lawmaking task, for it may make the balance come out against an otherwise desirable course of action.

A court may decide, on the other hand, to give guidance through specificity. In recent years courts have been more willing to take this path at the price of changing the traditional role of the court. On occasion, however, it may prove necessary to pay that price in order to allow a court to discharge its obligation to make the best law it can.

In summary, it can be seen that judicial ability to make law may in many circumstances equal or surpass that of the legislature. When that is not so, the court must face up to the possibility that clumsy intrusion into an area may cause more harm than good; a court must recognize these possibilities and take care to ameliorate unfortunate side effects when it issues opinions. The most important step, of course, is the exercise of great care in the formulation of new law. Close adherence in decision-making to doctrinal developments in other jurisdictions, and readiness to recognize and correct error also helps avoid or soften problems, for the experience in other jurisdictions can be a very valuable teacher.

Finally, judges should always remember that they do not represent the popular will in the way legislators do, a factor that should lead to the exercise of caution in the making of law, and, perhaps, even refusal to enter into new territory, a subject discussed in the next section.

§ 4.25 Judicial Abstention

Courts exist to decide cases. Not all claims brought before them are adjudicated, however. A number of doctrines have developed that limit the scope of judicial reach. Some of these relate to judicial power. An example is the requirement that a court have jurisdiction, both personal and subject matter, before it can decide a case. Other limiting concepts are designed to insure that the case is properly set up for adjudication. Thus, a plaintiff must have "standing" to bring the action—he must be someone "injured" by the defendant's conduct.

Beyond those requirements, the question remains whether a court may ever decline to pass on a case otherwise properly before it on the ground that the legislature could better resolve the question at hand (sometimes expressed in the form, "This is a job for the legislature"). Although some of the arguments for that position, as well as some of the responses to them, were exposed in the preceding section, two more arguments against judicial abstention will be discussed here.

The first is a practical argument: At least in traditional cases judges probably perform as well as the legislature. Consider the case of comparative negligence. For over a century the common law of torts rejected that doctrine, embracing instead the all-or-nothing rule of contributory negligence, albeit ameliorated somewhat by concepts such as last clear chance. In the 1960's courts began hearing cases which urged the adoption of comparative negligence. The initial judicial response was that the problem was one properly left to the legislature to solve. After all, such change involved a reversal of well established common-law principles and also raised several difficult questions (e.g., can a plaintiff who is more than 50% negligent recover anything?). Gradually, however, courts began to take a different view of the matter, and today a number of appellate courts have adopted comparative negligence as the governing standard for their systems. Their doing so was proper; because contributory negligence was a common-law development, it was the responsibility of the judges to oversee the growth, change, and even death of the doctrine they created. A hard-pressed legislature may not have time (or energy or political courage) to correct case law mistakes; consequently, for the judiciary to place that burden on them is an abdication of its responsibility.

As for competence, the doctrine of comparative negligence involves issues with which courts are intimately familiar and it is hard to imagine why the necessary elaboration could not be accomplished in the form of a judicial opinion. In fact, Robert Leflar, after surveying legislative developments, found that legislative law in this area was not any better than could be expected of judicial law. Leflar, Comment on Maki v. Frelk, 21 Vand.

L.Rev. 906 (1968). Further, a court that decides an issue after some legislatures have tried to cope with the problem may be guided by the experiences of those legislatures. The lawmaker who first forges into an area may not see all of the problems that may arise from a proposed solution; that is the price a pioneer must pay. But in good common law fashion, a court can shape and reshape its decisions in order to eliminate those difficulties.

Support for judicial lawmaking is found in the fact that legislatures apparently consider courts capable of handling extremely difficult problems going to the root of our social and economic structure. The evidence for that observation comes from the legislative proclivity to adopt open-ended statutes whose general admonitions resemble the most amorphous judicial pronouncement. Almost all of antitrust law can be placed in that category, as can the majestic phrases of the Civil Rights Act of 1866. Such statutes, frequently encountered, demonstrate the confidence of the legislature in the ability of the courts to handle lawmaking with little more guidance than, "Do good in the area of business mergers; prevent some but not all of them."

The second argument against judicial abstention is theoretical. Our courts exist to decide disputes among litigants. The legislature confers jurisdiction upon courts to hear cases. The expectation is that if no statutory or constitutional law is involved, and if the dispute falls within the court's jurisdiction, that body will decide the problem using its lawmaking power. Abstention, therefore, would be a failure to perform up to expectations concerning the proper role of the judiciary.

That response may be too facile. The expectations sketched above developed as judges engaged in traditional decision making involving claims of right between two parties, claims that could be settled fairly effectively by decree. Professor Abram Chayes, in The Role of the Judge in Public Law Litigation, 89 Harv.L.Rev. 1281 (1976), labeled that the "bipolar" model. The pressure to reach a decision in a "bipolar" case can be seen easily. The bipolar model also disciplines judicial lawmaking for the decision itself has an immediate impact upon the parties. Because the court can usually gauge that impact from the facts before it, the immediacy of the dispute and of its resolution push the court towards making the best law that it can.

Recent years have seen a trend away from the traditional bipolar dispute, particularly in constitutional and administrative law. Prominent causes have been the relaxation of standing requirements and willingness to innovate in granting equitable relief. Judges today sometimes take charge of school systems (including their financing) and prisons, reapportion legislatures, and supervise the hiring of new police.

This activism has not been universally popular. Many have argued that judges act improperly in opening up new territory, that they should not decide cases in areas where societal values have not had a chance to take definite form, a problem compounded by the indeterminate effect of the creative remedies that sometimes must be imposed to implement the new doctrine. Because many persons believe that such choices should be made by the more representative legislature, and that courts are not equal to the new demands placed on them, there is substantial sentiment in favor of restricting courts to the bipolar model. Others, of course, have hailed judicial willingness to intervene where a properly presented claim of right is brought before them. At present, no consensus on this issue has emerged. It is a problem that every student of the judicial process should bear in mind.

Finally, the problem of judicial abstention should be separated from a decision not to recognize a claim of right on its merits. Consider the case of a person who sues a private association, for example, alleging that it expelled her in violation of its own rules. A court probably will not listen to that claim unless it sees some contract or property right implicated by the situation. Instead, the judges will give effect to another valued principle, private group autonomy, and deny the cause of action. That decision is not based, however, on a belief that the court should not make law, but, rather, is based on an analysis of the wisdom of interfering in the internal affairs of private organizations. When the private activity does involve important societal interests, the court will intervene. E.g., Falcone v. Middlesex County Medical Soc. (1961).

§ 4.26 Judicial Discretion

Judges and commentators often refer to a judge's exercise of "discretion." Although the term implies a freedom to choose on the judge's part, that does not really help us understand problems connected with judicial discretion. That is because the term "discretion" is used to refer to several fairly distinct types of events, and the various usages must be sorted out in order to discuss the questions of whether and how a judge exercises discretion. (A short and incisive discussion of discretion has been written by Prof. Ronald Dworkin, The Model of Rules, 35 U.Chi.L.Rev. 14, 32–34 (1967)).

On some occasions a court is said to have discretion because it is not expected either to justify its decision or to make it consistent with other decisions. The clearest example of this is the decision to deny certiorari. As noted earlier (§ 3.11), courts, due to "practical considerations," are not expected to justify such a decision, and the standards to be applied are both non-reviewable and generally so loose as to be meaningless. Still, even in this area there *are* standards, hemming in to some extent the judge's freedom to act. But the sheer volume of certiorari petitions to most courts makes uniformity and justification difficult, if not impossible.

The term discretion is also used to refer to the fact that a court's decision cannot be reviewed by anyone else. The decision of the highest court of a state on a problem not involving federal law is the end of the line for that case. Thus, that court can choose the policies to apply to the dispute, how those policies work, and so on. As used in this context, "discretion" has little bearing on *how* a court should function; it refers instead to the reality of power exercised by a judge. That power does not exist unchecked. Although a court of last resort may be free of effective formal checks, it does not necessarily follow that that court is free to "do as it chooses." The court operates within a great many institutional constraints, among them the need to engage in reasoned elaboration (§ 4.7), the need to explain a decision in public and in writing (§ 3.1), and the need generally to satisfy the hardlearned demands of the judge's craft. Thus, it can be said that although a judge of a court of last resort is "free" to choose, in practice the "freedom" is limited. The path a judge must tread is carefully circumscribed, and the deviations permitted relatively few in number. Even when one of those is taken, the judicial profession compels the judge to explain the decision in a fashion that will satisfy the most caustic of commentators as to why that was the one chosen.

Another use of the term "discretion" indicates that a judge has considerable leeway in making a decision in the sense that the judge will not be reversed unless "clearly" wrong. So used, "discretion" (often referred to as "sound discretion") seems to be a substitute for "judgment" or "wisdom." In a number of areas judges are said to exercise discretion in this sense, and in these areas the exercise of judicial discretion is generally accepted. Prominent among those classes is sentencing in criminal cases (at least in some jurisdictions), the grant of equitable relief, and the choice of certain procedural devices, such as a new trial. In many jurisdictions, a judge performing any of those functions is under no formal compulsion to explain the decision or to relate that decision to others made within the jurisdiction or elsewhere. (Review of these decisions by a higher court centers on whether the judge below has "abused" his discretion, a difficult inquiry because there generally are no standards that explain how discretion can be abused.)

It is difficult to understand the survival of discretion in these areas; the explanations for its survival appear to be grounded partly on history, partly on the unwillingness of trial judges to take the time to explain their decisions, and partly on the reluctance by appellate judges to establish rules that would permit them to review some of the more difficult decisions made by a trial judge. In addition, because the trial judge was close to the situation and weighed many intangible factors in reaching a decision, appellate judges do not feel comfortable second-guessing the trial judge. There is, however, pressure in some of those traditionally "discretionary" areas to reduce the leeway afforded a sentencing judge—for example, by making the judge explain the sentence given and providing a mechanism for effective appellate review of sentencing decisions. We give our judges great power, but that does not mean they should operate without the institutional constraints that make each decision law.

Finally, it can be asked whether judges exercise "discretion" when they make law, that is, when they decide which principles to establish for future use, or is choice foreclosed by the combination of precedent and the craft of common law judges? That problem is too complex to examine here. It can be noted, however, that, in practice, making the "correct" decision in some areas must depend on the wisdom and common sense of the tribunal. That is, those are decisions about which reasonable persons could differ. It should not be hard to understand why that is so. The establishment of any principle requires the evaluation of a large number of competing claims. The level of confidence in any judge's ability to appreciate the full impact of any of those claims cannot, in the nature of things, be very high; human problems do not lend themselves to categorical resolutions. For that reason, judges with different training may in good faith reach opposite results, for there can be real disagreement over such issues as the desirability of strict rules and the scope of a judge's lawmaking authority.

PART D
CHANGING THE COMMON LAW

One of the recurring problems a court must face concerns the continued validity of its precedent. A court is continually asked to examine the vitality and legitimacy of its earlier decisions. Three major questions present themselves in this area: should a court overrule itself, when should it do so, and should the overruling have retroactive effect. Inherent in these questions is the continuing problem of how best to reconcile the competing goals of stability and flexibility in decision-making.

§ 4.27   Should Cases Be Overruled

It would be possible to have a legal system based on a view of precedent that no decision should ever be overruled. Such a view is not held by American courts; they believe that they have the power to change their minds, cast out discredited, time-worn cases, and weave new decisions into the seamless web that is the law. For at least two-thirds of a century, however, the British House of Lords followed a strict rule of precedent; beginning with London Streets Tramways Co. v. London County Council, [1898], the Lords, despite authority to the contrary, formally renounced the power to overrule their own decisions. In 1966, however, the Lords announced, in a "Practice Statement," that they would feel free "to depart from a previous decision when it appears right to do so." Today, therefore, it can be said that no common law court feels absolutely bound by its own earlier decisions; of course, as discussed in § 2.2, the decisions of a higher court bind lower courts in the same judicial hierarchy. Nevertheless, it will be instructive to examine the arguments for a rigid system of precedent for the light that they cast on the general problems associated with the question of overruling.

a. Certainty

In the *London Tramways* case Lord Halsbury argued for a strict rule of *stare decisis* in part because of "the disastrous inconvenience of having each question subject to being reargued and the dealings of mankind rendered doubtful by reason of different decisions, so that in truth and in fact there would be no real final court of appeal." The appeal to the need for certainty is a common one among those who argue for a strict view of precedent. American judges also speak of the need for certainty. A typical plea for certainty is found in Alferitz v. Borgwardt (1899): "The mere fact that an error has been made in a decision * * * is no reason for perpetuating it, but in a given case to correct it may be productive of more evil than to permit it to stand * * *." From these quotes it can be seen that certainty has two component parts, finality and predictability.

There can be no doubt that the law has a very strong interest in certainty. Doctrines designed to achieve that end, such as law of the case, res judicata, and collateral estoppel, play a very important role in our jurisprudence. Certainty in the law also makes the court's job much easier, for a court would face an impossible burden if it were necessary to reexamine all the issues presented by a case. Yet judicial insistence on certainty exacts a price from the courts, the law, and society.

The most obvious of those costs is the harmful effect of a bad rule. Although the legislature always has the power to correct nonconstitutional judicial errors, it is silly to pretend that it has either the time or inclination to do so, or even that it is aware that those errors have been made. Consequently, a bad decision may live a long time, hampering the efficient and just functioning of society.

More subtle penalties are extracted as a result of strict adherence to precedent as the court itself tries to live with a bad decision. Rather than overrule it, many courts twist and turn in agony under its impact, using every device available to ingenious legal minds to whittle the decision down, to "distinguish" it, in order to limit its harmful effects. Often such efforts are seen—rightly—as designed to obliterate an opinion without formal overruling. In doing so, however, a court runs serious risks of undermining the belief in the integrity of its own decision-making, as those who must follow its decisions perceive that the court's attempted distinctions make no sense, or that the attempts at explanation could not survive a case-book editor's caustic comments. Such decision-making also forms bad habits for those who indulge in it, for the practice of rigorous and careful analysis is one that is not easily come by and can be quickly lost. Constant striving is necessary to maintain quality opinion writing.

If a court limits its opinions to soften the impact of a strict rule of *stare decisis* the range of the principles contained in the precedent is limited also. Broad considerations of policy are less likely to be isolated and used as the basis for later decision-making. Not surprisingly, therefore, a court that feels absolutely bound by its own pronouncements will become exceedingly cautious in making them. After all, it is much easier to expand a narrow statement than to distinguish honestly a broad one. Occasional broad statements of policy are important to the development of the law; thus, it is a disservice when the judicial process discourages a court from making them.

Worse, attempted distinctions and their attendant explanations can on their own create bad law. A gimcrack rationale may apparently save the day, but when a new problem arises, the attempt at explanation may itself lead to further trouble.

b. Predictability

Predictability, one of the virtues of certainty, deserves a separate discussion because of its importance. Whenever the law is uncertain, risk increases in a transaction and the cost of that transaction increases (see R. Posner, supra § 4.2). To put this argument more practically, an attorney advising a client tries to suggest courses of action that are likely to succeed; the more the advice must be hedged due to worry over the stability of case law in the area, the less value the advice has to the client. Further, uncertain case law often means more research by the attorney in an effort to understand which way the court will jump; the cost of that research will make the attorney's advice more expensive (or, in the alternative, if the research is not undertaken due to the expense, the advice will be more risky and less valuable).

One response to the predictability argument centers on the lack of precision of agreement among all the judges of a court. Our appellate courts face heavy caseloads and time does not permit the luxury of hammering out agreement among all judges on all points covered in the opinion. That inability to attain precision of agreement is fatal, however, to any system that would carve the judges' words into stone; to have the force of prophecy they must be written with steadier hands.

Another consideration involving predictability raises more problems in this country than in Britain. We have an immense number of courts in many different jurisdictions deciding many of the same legal issues. Yet we think of our law as somehow "national"—albeit with local idiosyncrasies—a belief reinforced by law schools, national legal encyclopedias, by a national Restatement of the Law in various areas, and so on. There exists a great deal of pressure on the courts to reconcile decisions in different jurisdictions. To do so, of course, a court must be free to change its mind and to modify or discard its earlier decisions. In addition, our citizens enter into a vast number of transactions in states other than the one where they live, transactions often involving more than one jurisdiction. Those dealings need the security afforded by a fairly universal law. In the absence of a single court such as the House of Lords that can oversee common law decision-making, the task of adapting the law in one jurisdiction to national trends can, again, be secured only if judges are not totally bound by what has occurred in the past.

Finally, predictability may be *enhanced* by over-ruling. Two conflicting lines of precedent may develop in an area leading to confusion that can be alleviated only by eliminating one of the lines.

c. *A Legislature's Job*

In Beamish v. Beamish (1861), relied on heavily by Lord Halsbury in *London Tramways,* Lord Campbell advanced a third argument in support of his belief that the House of Lords lacked power to overrule its own decision:

[T]he rule of law which your Lordships lay down as the ground of your judgment * * * must be taken for law till altered by an Act of Parliament * * *. The law laid down as your *ratio decidendi,* being clearly binding on all inferior tribunals * * * if it were not considered as equally binding upon your Lordships, this House would be arrogating to itself the right of altering the law, and legislating by its own separate authority.

Two responses can be made to that argument. First, a court "legislates" when it lays down any new rule; it is hard to see any significant difference between legislating the new rule and changing an old one. In both situations, it is a court, not a legislative body, that has said how it will control future actions.

More important, Lord Campbell's argument is based on the premise that courts should not override their prior decisions—that it is not proper in the political scheme of things for them to do so. The validity of the argument depends, therefore, on the accuracy of the political picture it presupposes. In American society, at least, we expect our judges to correct their errors and to keep the law in tune with the times. This has long been the practice in this country, understood and approved by the great majority familiar with the way our courts operate. However valid a strict regime of *stare decisis* may be for Great Britain, it does not correspond to American expectations.

d. *Efficiency*

A final argument for a tight view of precedent centers on judicial administration. A court hard-pressed for time must find a well-defined precedent a thing of beauty. It provides a rule which can be slapped on a case leading to a quick solution of the problem up for decision. Precedent, therefore, helps conserve expensive judicial resources.

The judicial efficiency argument generally resembles the arguments based on certainty and predictability. All things being equal, we do want to achieve justice with more speed and less expense. But all things are not equal because the costs associated with a bad precedent cannot be ignored. Judicial efficiency alone does not suffice to justify the policy of strict adherence to precedent, given the serious costs of that policy.

e. *Fairness*

Adherence to precedent also promotes consistency in decision-making. Like the other values associated with a regime of *stare decisis,* consistency and fairness are important. They are not, however, all important, and at times may be sacrificed in order to achieve other goals.

§ 4.28 When to Overrule

The steps a judge takes in deciding when to overrule precedent cannot be stated as an arithmetic equation. A judge contemplating such a decision must evaluate a number of intangible factors; often a judge has little information at his disposal concerning the weight of some or all of those factors.

The first step, of course, requires the judge to determine that the old rule was a mistake, or that society has changed since it was announced, or that the new rule simply works better. Here the judge uses the techniques discussed in Part C of this Chapter. Although deciding that establishing a new rule would better serve society is necessary to the decision to overrule, it is not in itself sufficient; the larger question of whether to overrule requires consideration of other societal interests, and whether those interests are sufficient to require adherence to a "wrong" decision.

The major factor to be considered in determining whether to overrule precedent is the value of a regime of *stare decisis* as discussed earlier (§ 4.11). Every overruling requires that a price be paid: loss of stability and confidence, damage to the efficiency of the system, reduction in predictability. A court must analyze these factors so that it can cast a balance on the profit or loss to be gained from overruling. Although some of the factors to be considered are relatively indeterminate in their effect, careful analysis can help resolve some of the problems.

A good example of analysis considering the factors involved in overruling is Moragne v. States Marine Lines, Inc. (1970) (also discussed in § 4.23).

There Justice Harlan overruled an earlier decision
to hold that an action for wrongful death would lie
in admiralty based on a shipowner's failure to
maintain a seaworthy vessel in territorial waters
(unseaworthiness is a less demanding standard for
a plaintiff to meet than that of common law negligence).   Relying on analysis by Hart and Sacks
(supra § 4.2), and others, Harlan pointed out that
under existing law failure to maintain a seaworthy
vessel would subject shipowners to liability in situations that closely resembled the one at bar.   Under those circumstances,

> it could hardly be said that shipowners have
> molded their conduct around the possibility that
> in a few special circumstances they may escape
> liability for such a breach.   Rather, the estab-
> lished expectations of both those who own ships
> and those who work on them are that there is a
> duty to make the ship seaworthy and that a
> breach of that federally imposed duty will gener-
> ally provide a basis for recovery.   It is the excep-
> tional denial of recovery that disturbs these ex-
> pectations.

Overruling would not, therefore, unfairly surprise
the owners by changing retroactively their standard of conduct;   that is, it would not change their
duty of care owed the longshoremen.   Futher, overruling would also harmonize the law in the area.

In *Moragne* the court also discussed the question
of the effects of overruling precedent on judicial
efficiency.   Harlan pointed out that the rule being

overturned "has become an increasingly unjustifiable anomaly * * * and * * * has produced litigation-spawning confusion in an area that should be susceptible of more workable solutions." The old rule, that is, had led to confusion; the new one might be able to put those problems to rest. Overruling a precedent, in other words, may enhance judicial efficiency, especially in those situations in which a patently bad rule has driven courts to efforts to avoid its impact.

It is sometimes argued that predictability is more important in some areas than in others. Generally, where planning for future events is involved—in drafting a will, for example, or reorganizing a corporation—predictability can be quite significant, due to the fact that instruments such as wills or trust agreements that are drawn up today may not be given legal effect for several decades. If there were no stability in the law, estate planning would become virtually impossible. Careful analysis of the situation must still be made, however, for cases may arise in which the value of stability is relatively slight.

Careful analysis of the bases of precedent and their application to the case at bar can provide a great deal of guidance to a court faced with the decision whether to follow or overrule precedent. Further, it would seem that *stare decisis* requires at least a good showing of ultimate benefit to society before the system may be disrupted by an overruling; the proponents of change, in other words, must bear the burdens of proof and persuasion. In the end, however, a court must be willing to discard the old rule when those burdens have been met. To quote Chief Justice Vanderbilt in Fox v. Snow (1950):

> The question whether the doctrine of *stare decisis* should be adhered to * * * is always a choice between relative evils. When it appears that the evil resulting from a continuation of the accepted rule must be productive of greater mischief to the community than can possibly ensue from disregarding the previous adjudications on the subject, courts have frequently and wisely departed from precedent.

§ 4.29 Prospective Overruling

The past thirty years have witnessed widespread consideration of a new issue in judicial decision-making: whether to apply a new doctrine in the traditionally retroactive way, or to apply it prospectively only. Although the problem is presented most starkly when case law is overruled, it can be raised whenever a court adopts or changes doctrine.

The question of retroactivity did not occur to writers on the common law such as Blackstone who argued for a "declaratory" theory of law. Under that theory, a decision was not law, but was merely evidence of law. Thus Blackstone: "if it be found that the former decision is manifestly absurd or unjust, it is declared, not that such was bad law, but that it was not law * * * " 1 Commentaries *70. A decision, therefore, could be "wrong," but the law was not; it had merely been expressed imperfectly in the decision. Because the law always existed, the question of prospective decision-making was not addressed by adherents of the declaratory theory. American judges, however, by the middle of the last century began to realize that in certain situations retroactive decision-making imposed unfair hardships. As a result, prospective overruling began to be adopted. Today, it is a technique used by many courts, an issue explored in this section.

Consider the case of charitable immunity. For a long period in the nineteenth and twentieth centuries charitable institutions enjoyed general immunity for torts committed by their agents. The primary reason for this immunity was to maximize the ability of the charity to perform good deeds. Three decades ago courts began to understand that the justification, even if sensible on its face, could not compete with the need to make every organization pay its own way (internalize costs) and the need to recompense tort victims. When it came time to eliminate the doctrine, however, courts realized that many charities, apparently relying on their judicial grant of non-liability, did not carry insurance. To impose full tort liability, therefore, might bankrupt a charity. How should a court proceed?

The first point, of course, is to determine the desirability of the old rule. Assuming that it would be thought unwise, if the case were one of first impression, to grant the immunity, the problem then becomes the quality and extent of reliance on the old rule. The *new* decision to abolish the immunity may have been so clearly foreshadowed by other decisions that a court may well feel no hesitation in overruling a doctrine with complete retroactivity. See, e.g., Muskopf v. Corning Hosp. Dist. (1961).

The new rule may, however, be "a clear break with the past," Desist v. United States (1969), and the court must then consider the quality of the reliance on the precedent. As discussed in the preceding section, the reliance by the charity on the doctrine of immunity, like that of the shipowner in *Moragne,* can be seen as remedial, and would not, therefore, raise problems of the same magnitude as those that occur when there is reliance on a rule having an impact on how a person behaves. Yet many courts have agonized over the imposition of liability on the charity. The reason, of course, is that the charity has relied—and relied heavily—on the precedent establishing immunity. The reliance took the form of not purchasing insurance to cover liability. It is not surprising that courts have hesitated to abolish by judicial fiat charitable immunity.

One way around the problem is to announce in the case at bar that in the *next* case involving a similar cause of action arising after the date of decision of the present case the doctrine of immunity will be abandoned. This is known as prospective overruling. An eminently practical course, this method of solving the problem is one that has been adopted by a number of courts faced with decisions in both the area of charitable immunity and the related problem of governmental immunity. It is also a solution that has been rejected by many courts. As might be expected, commentators are also on both sides of the issue. An understanding of the problem will be helped by discussing the arguments made in opposition to prospective overruling.

a. Constitutional Problems

One set of objections raises questions based on constitutional doctrine. The Supreme Court has made it clear that prospective decision-making does not violate the due process clauses of the Fifth and Fourteenth Amendments to the United States Constitution. The gist of the due process argument is that a party who loses a case due to a prospective decision has had liberty or property taken without due process of law. The leading case rejecting that argument is Great Northern Ry. Co. v. Sunburst Oil & Refining Co. (1932); because of that decision cases having prospective effect are sometimes referred to as "*Sunbursts.*"

b. Dictum

This objection is more telling. The fundamental premise that underpins the assertion of a common law court that it has power to make law is the need to invoke law to decide the case before it. If the decision does not flow from the opinion, then the latter is *dictum* (see § 4.14), because the language of the opinion was not necessary to dispose of the case. Hence, it would seem the very antithesis of common law decision-making to apply a decision prospectively; that is, to announce that a new policy will apply in the future, but in the case at bar—the one that brought the issue to the attention of the court—another policy will control. In short, the power to make law has been separated from the need to decide cases.

The usual response to the *dictum* argument, developed best by then Professor (and now Judge) Robert Keeton in Prospective Judicial Lawmaking (1969), emphasizes the indeterminacy of all precedent. We have discussed earlier (§ 4.13) the idea that the shape and scope of precedent can only be seen as the case is interpreted and reformulated by later courts; it can be truly said, therefore, that the full effect of *any* decision operates prospectively. It is also common for judges to give examples of how a rule should operate through the use of hypothetical applications; this, too, is a form of prospective decision-making. Finally, the practice of writing separate opinions can be viewed as a practice of expressing ideas inconsistent with those in the majority, ideas that may one day, moreover, attract a majority of their own.

The second response to the *dictum* argument centers on an evaluation of the court's role in a rapidly changing society such as ours. For better or worse, our courts have thought it necessary to respond to rapidly changing social conditions by constantly modifying and changing case law. Some of the shifts can have a dramatic impact upon those who have planned and acted on the basis of old law. Although it is easy to say that charities, for example, should have foreseen a shift away from immunity and to tort liability, a court must find it very difficult to issue an opinion that may bankrupt some charities, unless the probability of its doing so should clearly have been foreseen. In contrast, judges a century ago may have believed that their opinions mirrored widely shared and deeply held values of reasonably stable societies. In addition, the widely held notion of Blackstone that law always *exists,* waiting for a court to find it, discouraged a push to prospective decision-making. The reliance argument was, accordingly, not felt as keenly, for a decision announcing a "new" rule did not change the law. Our own perception that judges do make law leads, on the other hand, to appreciation of reliance on the old rule. That appreciation, in turn, helps push a court towards the use of prospective decision-making.

c. Respect

Related to the dictum argument is one advanced in Mishkin, Foreword: The High Court, The Great Writ, and the Due Process of Time and Law, 79 Harv.L.Rev. 56 (1965). Professor Mishkin's argument builds on recognition of the political reality of a court's power; the court depends on its prestige, primarily among the bar, to insure that it speaks with an effective voice in society. To the extent that judicial prestige depends upon the court's maintaining a traditional approach to decision-making, there are obvious problems with prospective decision-making. Once again, this is an argument that can be turned on its head, for one can argue as easily that disrespect comes with the "unfair" imposition of old rules, as would be the case in the charitable immunity situation. A rough evaluation suggests that there is a good deal of merit to Mishkin's point; the bar, because of its training in, and long use of *stare decisis,* feels uneasy with prospective overruling. Some use of the device does seem acceptable to the bar, however, and it is up to the court to convince its audience of the need for its use in a particular case.

d. Restraint

A more telling argument against prospective decision-making, although still related to the one just discussed, focuses on the functional role played by the traditional requirement that decisions operate retroactively. A retroactive decision has immediate impact; the court is aware of—and considers—the impact not only on the case at bar but on all other similar situations throughout its jurisdiction. That consideration is important because courts generally have played a modest role in our government; they legislate, in Justice Holmes' famous phrase, "interstitially."

Prospective decision-making may lessen the pressures that have led to that modest role, for the court that engages in it, like a legislature, need not worry about how the decision will affect events that already have taken place. Instead, the court is free to remodel society without the restraints imposed by completed events. Those restraints are powerful; to override them a court has to be very sure that what it is doing not only makes sense, but represents society's principles so clearly that reliance on old law properly can be set aside.

The restraint argument is a strong one and certainly runs against a court that would engage in widespread prospective decision-making. If that technique is reserved for compelling, extraordinary cases, however—with express recognition that the technique should be so reserved—then the court runs less risk that its conduct will be viewed as falling outside the court's proper role. This approach allows prospective decision-making to be available when needed.

e. A Practical Objection

Another frequently voiced objection to prospective decision-making argues that a likely effect of that technique will be to discourage litigants from raising fundamental issues. What incentive does a litigant or attorney have to raise a new issue, expending time and money in the process, if it will not bring victory? Such an effect, of course, would be most unfortunate; it is imperative that questions such as the continued immunity of charities from tort liability be freely raised before courts. It is doubtful, however, that prospective decision-making seriously discourages litigants from raising such questions. A court may, after all, make a decision fully retroactive. Often, too, there is no alternative available but to make the argument; if you have been hit by a truck owned by a charity and the driver is judgment-proof (or immune), you have little choice but to question charitable immunity and convince the court to apply any change retroactively. Finally, an institutional litigant may be quite satisfied with a prospective ruling if the institution has a number of cases that raise the same issue; it has achieved the principle it wants and financial victory will come later.

Still, courts have worried that without the carrot of total success issues may not be raised. It also is somewhat difficult to pat the head of the person crippled by the charity's truck and say "Nice argument, too bad you get nothing from it." One response to those pressures is to make the decision retroactive *only* in the case at bar.

Unfortunately, that solution raises a major problem of its own, for it violates the principle that like cases should be decided in like fashion. Consider two plaintiffs, Jack and Jill, injured in the same accident by the truck of a charity. Jack's case comes before the court first; it announces that charities no longer will be immune in tort, but that the decision will not be applied to any torts arising before the date of the decision other than in Jack's own case. This eliminates any chance that Jill, who has not yet had a hearing, has of recovering. Although it is possible to argue, as the courts in fact do, that the situations can be distinguished on the need to reward the plaintiff and, at the same time, protect those charities that have not yet purchased insurance, it will be difficult to convince Jill that the principle of consistency has not been violated in her case.

Still, courts have not hesitated to employ the technique of overruling with only partial prospectivity. A typical explanation is Stovall v. Denno (1967), in which the Supreme Court decided the question of the effect to be given United States v. Wade (1967), and Gilbert v. California (1967) (*Wade* and *Gilbert* had held that an accused had a right to counsel at a pre-trial confrontation):

> We recognize that *Wade* and *Gilbert* are, therefore, the only victims of pretrial confrontations in the absence of their counsel to have the bene-

fit of the rules established in their cases. That they must be given that benefit, is, however, an unavoidable consequence of the necessity that constitutional adjudications not stand as mere dictum * * * Inequity arguably results from according the benefit of a new rule to the parties in the case in which it is announced but not to other litigants similarly situated in the trial or appellate process who have raised the same issue. But we regard the fact that the parties involved are chance beneficiaries as an insignificant cost for adherence to sound principles of decision-making.

To sum up, prospective over-ruling raises a number of difficult institutional and practical difficulties. It seems clear, however, that our courts will continue to employ it, albeit with some hesitation.

§ 4.30 A Concluding Word

In rendering a decision a judge must be aware that its impact will be both present (the litigants in the case), and future (those whose activities will be affected by the decision). The decision, therefore, must be one that the judge is prepared to apply to future cases as well as the one before the court. In order to show the fairness of the decision and help others to understand it, the opinion must explain what goals it is seeking to achieve and how the opinion will do that. Similarly, in evaluating precedents from other courts, the judge determines the purposes motivating those decisions and whether the purposes would be advanced by application in the instant case. If they would be advanced the judge must finally decide whether those policies still are worthy of protection. If not, the judge must then decide whether to overrule; whether the cost of doing so (especially to those who relied on the precedent) exceeds the cost that a bad rule imposes on society. The search is one for wisdom and justice; it should be a public search, both to reassure and to educate.

CHAPTER FIVE
STATUTORY INTERPRETATION
PART A
UNDERSTANDING THE TASK
§ 5.1 Overview

A "statute," as used in this *Nutshell,* is a term applied to the formal enactment, following constitutional procedures, of the legislative component of a sovereign body. Both Houses of Congress, for example, must approve a bill. It is then either signed by the President or passed over his veto. When that process is completed the bill becomes a statute. A similar process occurs in every state. A statute should be distinguished from other legislative expressions such as a committee report; it should also be distinguished from an "ordinance," a term which usually refers to enactments by the legislative body of a subordinate governmental unit—a county or municipal council, for example.

The fundamental principle of statutory interpretation is that a statute is enacted by a body that has law-making power superior to a court (except in matters of constitutional law). Judicial power is limited to interpreting legislation in the course of deciding cases. A realist might scoff at that formal explanation, however, for the legislature does not apply its laws, it merely passes them. As Bishop Hoadly told George I in 1717, "whoever hath an absolute authority to *interpret* any written or spoken laws, it is *he* who is truly the *Law giver* to all intents and purposes, and not the person who first wrote or spoke them." *Quoted in* J. Gray, The Nature and Sources of the Law 125 (2d ed. 1921). Many writers have agreed with Bishop Hoadly that the authority of a statute comes ultimately from the manner in which it is interpreted by the judges. Under this view a statute is evidence of what the law is—persuasive evidence, to be sure— but not *law* until interpreted and applied by a court.

Although that pragmatic observation may appear well-founded, it must be remembered that most judges believe in the concept of legislative supremacy. Their decision-making generally is predicated on that belief, and statutory interpretation, therefore, is dominated by judicial recognition of the primary role of the legislature.

The question for a court, then, is how best to recognize and give effect to legislative desires. This Chapter begins by examining several possible methods of approaching interpretive questions. It then considers possible aids to interpretation (such as legislative history), and concludes with an examination of special problems in interpretation. Dominating all aspects of the inquiry is the paramount role of the legislative voice.

Bibliography. In addition to the sources cited in § 1.1, and in the course of this chapter, Professor Reed Dickerson's, The Interpretation and Application of Statutes (1975), is a perceptive analysis emphasizing the theoretical aspects of the subject. An excellent casebook is Eskridge and Frickey's Cases and Materials on Legislation (1988). The several volumes of J. Sutherland, Statutes and Statutory Construction (4th ed. D. Sands, 1986), provide good discussion and a very useful compilation of case law; in addition, a number of leading articles are reproduced. Sir Rupert Cross, in Statutory Interpretation (1976), provides an interesting and detailed analysis of British law and thought on interpretation.

§ 5.2 Why a Theory?

There are good reasons for courts to articulate (and use) an interpretive theory. The first is consistency in decision-making. Although there are several widely used theories of interpretation, courts vary in their application of them. Courts will often use none of these theories. On occasion they will invoke several. In many opinions it appears that the judges have worked out the result in advance and then reached for a theory that purports to justify the decision. Rare is the opinion that works at establishing a theory of interpretation for the case at bar, one that will also help decide future cases. No wonder then that decisions on questions of interpretation often appear contradictory or *ad hoc*. Without an articulated method of interpretation, steadied by a good theoretical anchor, a court can reach inconsistent results through indiscriminate use of any data and arguments that strike its fancy. If a court has not elaborated, in advance, a model of decision-making that it will follow, it leaves itself open to the charge that its approach in a particular case has been geared to the justification of a particular result, without regard either to consistent or rational use of interpretive aids. Adherence to a previously elaborated model reduces its vulnerability to such charges. In short, a theory of interpretation encourages (and may be indispensable to) reasoned and neutral decision making (see § 4.7).

An interpretive theory also enhances predictability and aids planning. Lawyers for a client engaged in a commercial venture need to be certain of the interpretation that will be given controlling statutes; to do that they must know how that problem will be approached by all the courts in a judicial system. Hence, an articulated theory of interpretation reduces risk—a highly desirable goal. A statute expresses a desire by the legislature concerning what should be done. Its command must be implemented in numerous small decisions by businesses, counsel, and lower court judges, all of whom need to be instructed by the court as to how *it* will implement legislative desires. If the court does not properly perform that task it is to that extent frustrating the legislature's efforts. That can and should be avoided.

§ 5.3   The Task of the Court: General

The first section of this Chapter established the role of the court when questions of statutory interpretation arise: the job of the court is to give practical effect to the statute. That response neatly begs the real question in interpretation: exactly what *is* the "effect" of the statute and how does a court go about answering that question? Those are difficult questions, but answering them does depend in large part on recognizing the role the court should play in this area. The task of the judges is not to rewrite the statute as they would have written it, but to implement the legislative will and help to achieve its goal.

This point seems elementary, yet it has enormous implications. Nor has it met with universal acceptance. One reason is occasional judicial hostility toward legislative "interference." Judicial jealousy or resentment of legislative intrusion into what previously has been the exclusive preserve of the judiciary may lead to grudging judicial acceptance of a subordinate role. Another reason for occasional rejection of legislative primacy may be judicial dislike of the particular piece of legislation before the court. Judges have often been accused of rewriting a statute to achieve "better" ends. Commentators and judges alike have expressed concern that such was the motivation for a particular decision. One manifestation of this attitude can be seen in a well-known article by Justice

Brennan, State Constitutions and the Protection of Individual Rights, 90 Harv.L.Rev. 429 (1976), in which he urged state courts to use state constitutional provisions to protect civil liberties and civil rights. He did not, however, urge the state courts to try to ascertain what were the goals of those who drafted the constitutions, nor did he express any concern that judicial interpretation be consistent with those goals.

It is unfortunate that judicial hostility can lead a court to "rewrite" a statute. Judicial opinions must strive to acknowledge the primacy of legislative action and apply the statute to further the legislative goals.

§ 5.4 The Task of the Court: Theories

a. The Literal Approach

Because the legislature, when it acts, has primary authority, it might be thought that the best method for a court to use in interpreting a statute would be a literal approach. In other words, the court should read the language of the act and ascertain, without reference to any outside source (other than perhaps a dictionary and the preamble and other sections of the statute under consideration) the "plain meaning" of that language. In that way the court would minimize its intrusion into the legislative product. An expression of that belief can be found in Regina v. City of London Court Judge (1892): "if the words of an Act are clear, you must follow them, even though they lead to a manifest absurdity. The Court has nothing to do with whether the legislature has committed an absurdity." In theory, at least, this approach has attracted the attention of a number of courts, and was particularly popular in England in the Nineteenth Century. One reason for that popularity was the strong belief by the English courts in the law-making primacy of Parliament.

Paradoxically, the literal rule also attracted adherents because it *limited* the scope of legislation. For that reason, literalness was prevalent in this country at the turn of the present century, when judicial hostility toward the legislature reached its peak.

Another supposed advantage of literal interpretation is that it makes easier the task of those who must determine the statute's meaning. Not only can a business person presumably grasp the meaning of a statute by "looking" at it, he can also be confident of that interpretation because other sources of meaning (e.g., legislative history) are foreclosed from consideration.

Those advantages have led some judges, notably Justice Scalia, to indorse a literal approach. American courts in recent years, however, have generally although by no means universally rejected a literal approach. Several major reasons can be cited for that rejection:

Legislative Reality. A statute is often drafted in a hurry, perhaps without the help of counsel.

Worse, it may have been drafted orally on the floor. Many legislators are not lawyers, and thus are not conscious of the need to write with attention partly focused on how a court will respond. In those conditions it is quite likely that drafting errors will be made and clarity of meaning lost; hence, it is ludicrous to read a statute drafted under those conditions in the same fashion as one might read a document drawn up after weeks of effort by a team of top-flight attorneys. The more complex the statute the more likely this is to be true, suggesting that perhaps the literal rule worked better in an earlier age when legislation was simpler. It is important, therefore, that other aids to interpretation be used. For these reasons some courts believe that legislators, aware of the difficulty of doing their job properly, would tell a court to "do what we *tried* to do," and to make reasonable efforts to find out what that was.

Flexibility. A statute controls those situations that come within its ambit. In a rapidly changing society such as ours a legislative enactment may be called upon to handle situations far different from those contemplated at the time of its passage. If a statute is to deal successfully with those situations, it is necessary that the language of the statute be written with some flexibility. This is particularly important in the case of an enactment that is designed to respond to changing conditions. Article 2 of the Uniform Commercial Code (discussed in § 5.23) is a good example, for it emphasizes the legality and efficacy of reasonable commercial practices. Deliberate vagueness is also used to give agencies room to be flexible while responding to problems. Section 5 of the Federal Trade Commission Act, for example, gives the FTC power to outlaw "unfair methods of competition"—hardly a phrase where a literal interpretation will provide much guidance.

Precedent. The literal approach ignores the fact that a statute does not retain its pristine state as passed by the legislature. Judicial decisions soon put a gloss on it, a gloss that for reasons of consistency and reliance a court cannot ignore. The impact of *stare decisis* on interpretation mandates, therefore, that anyone interested in knowing the effect that a statute will be given consult material beyond the bare language of the statute. Even if courts have faithfully applied "literal" meaning, their opinions must be read to insure that fact.

Language. Any inquiry into "meaning" must recognize the need to look at language in context. No word has an "ideal" meaning, fixed and invariable over the span of human thought. Justice Holmes, as usual, put this observation in its most memorable form: "A word is not a crystal, transparent and unchanged, it is the skin of a living thought and may vary greatly in color and content according to the circumstances and the time in which it is used." Towne v. Eisner (1918).

Today, almost all lawyers are sophisticated in this respect and recognize the need to place language in context before it can be properly understood.　Routine admission of custom to interpret contractual language reflects widespread judicial acceptance of the idea that language cannot properly be interpreted without reference to the context in which it is used.　The phrase "community of interpretation" (derived from the philosopher Josiah Royce) has been used to express this concept;　language is used by a group to express thoughts and ideas, and to comprehend what that group was trying to express, it is necessary to appreciate how that community uses language.

If, therefore, language must be evaluated in context, a literal approach to interpretation must be rejected, for a court cannot be certain, without appreciation of the context, of the "literal" interpretation that should be placed on the words.　Appreciation of the context requires that a court be willing to consider evidence other than that contained in the bare bones of the statute.　As Learned Hand wrote, "There is no surer way to misread any document than to read it literally." Guiseppi v. Walling (1944).

b. *The Golden Rule*

The difficulties encountered in using the literal method of interpretation encouraged a search for ways to ameliorate its effect.　One response was what has come to be known as the "Golden Rule" of interpretation.　In Grey v. Pearson (1857), Baron Parke said that in construing written instruments, the grammatical and ordinary sense of the words is to be adhered to, unless that would lead to some absurdity, or some repugnancy or inconsistency with the rest of the instrument, in which case the grammatical and ordinary sense of the words may be modified so as to avoid the absurdity and inconsistency but no further.

The Golden Rule adds to the literal rule the idea that the legislature would not want its work construed so as to reach an "absurd" result. The Golden Rule represents, therefore, the general notion that statutes are to be construed as the work of a reasonable body trying to accomplish decent results. Although the legislature can accomplish unreasonable or "absurd" results, courts will make very sure of the legislature's desire to reach that result before they attribute such a meaning to a statute passed by a co-equal branch of government.

c. The Mischief Rule

The Golden Rule helps adjust interpretation to reality. Unfortunately, it obscures the major problem a court faces in applying the rule: How does a judge know when a result is "absurd"? Doubtless, an "absurd" result is "obvious," but again that answer assumes that a court can isolate such a result by looking at the statute and applying common knowledge. A more fundamental problem is that of seeking meaning in isolation, without inquiry into the goals of the statute. That kind of inquiry is central to full satisfaction of legislative desires, for if a court does not seek to ascertain fully what the legislature was trying to achieve, interpretation of the statute will only coincide with legislative goals fortuitously.

To say this somewhat differently, the legislature uses language in a statute only as means to an end, the achievement of some purpose. The words are that body's device for stating that purpose, to be sure, but they are not an end in themselves. Hence, statutory interpretation should focus on establishing the purpose or goal of the statute, rather than in analyzing the language used.

Courts have long recognized this need. As early as 1574, in Heydon's Case, as reported by Sir Edward Coke, the Barons of the Exchequers made the following resolutions:

> And it was resolved by them that for the sure and true interpretation of all statutes in general (be they penal or beneficial, restrictive or enlarging of the common law,) four things are to be discerned and considered:
>
> 1st.　What was the common law before the making of the Act.
>
> 2nd.　What was the mischief and defect for which the common law did not provide.
>
> 3rd.　What remedy the Parliament hath resolved and appointed to cure the disease of the commonwealth.
>
> And 4th.　The true reason of the remedy; and then the office of all the Judges is always to

make such construction as shall suppress
the mischief, and advance the remedy, and
to suppress subtle inventions and evasions
for continuance of the mischief, and *pro
privato commodo,* and to add force and life
to the cure and remedy, according to the
true intent of the makers of the Act, *pro
bono publico.*

Heydon's Case recognized that a statute represents the effort of a presumably reasonable body,
the legislature, to achieve certain goals.   (That
presumption may not seem to some always to be
well grounded in fact; it would appear, however, to
be quasi-constitutional in nature, reflecting the
proper respect owed by one branch of government
to another.)   The statute, then, has certain *purposes,* and the words of the act are the legislature's
way of attempting to control conduct down the
corridors of time.   It is through those words that
the legislature speaks to future generations.   Thus,
the job of the court is to try as best it can to
recognize and fulfill those purposes when it applies
the statute.

The resolutions reported by Lord Coke in Heydon's Case have come to be known as the "mischief" rule.   Under that approach the court's job is
to search out the defects in the old law that led to
the enactment and construe it so as to "suppress
the mischief and advance the remedy."   The purpose of the legislature in passing the statute, in
other words, is to be revealed by searching out the

problem in the law that led the legislature to attempt to change it.

d. The Purpose of the Statute

The mischief rule, despite its attractiveness, was generally superceded by less sophisticated methods such as the literal approach. A curious amalgam of reasons underlay this shift. In addition to the ones discussed earlier in this section and in § 5.6, there was, at least in this country, insufficient pressure on the courts to maintain a theory of interpretation. Legislatures did not pass many statutes and most of those that were adopted were relatively straight-forward, fairly easy of application, and, hence, relatively susceptible to a literal approach. Because most judicial business was non-statutory in nature, the courts were able to deal with matters of interpretation on an *ad hoc* (perhaps they might have said "common sense") basis. All this changed, however, when the great age of social reform through legislation began near the end of the last century. Because much of the thinking on the subject was generated by the work of the federal courts, two of the names associated with a modern approach to interpretation are Hand and Frankfurter; not surprisingly, both are also associated with judicial deference to legislative action.

Both judges emphasized the need for a court, when interpreting a statute, to place it in the context of its adoption so as to understand the goals the legislature had when it passed the law; the court should then construe the act so as to achieve statutory ends. Later scholars, especially Hart & Sacks (see § 4.2), building on such thoughts, used "purpose" when writing about proper methods of statutory interpretation as a technical term to explain what the interpreter should be seeking to establish. Today, American scholars generally follow their lead.

In practice the "purpose" approach asks that the court inquire into the legislature's goals in passing the statute, goals objectively defined, that are more general than the application to a particular situation; once those goals have been defined, the statute should be applied so as best to satisfy them. With most statutes the identification of purpose is a relatively simple task. All would agree that a statute that abolishes the Rule in Shelley's Case has as its purpose the elimination of a trap for the unwary in the conveyance of property. A purpose clause in a statute can also be helpful. But the search for purpose can be much more difficult.

Consider a statute that limits the number of bars that are permitted to operate in residential neighborhoods. It is quite possible that those who voted for that law had different purposes in doing so: to keep down noise, to enforce sobriety, to increase the value of existing taverns. All of those purposes may have motivated some legislators, and some may have been motivated by only one. Finding a majority purpose in this situation may be problematic. Perhaps all that can be said is that the statute has the purpose of limiting the number of bars, for that is all that a reasonable observer could distill from the evidence as a commonly held goal of the statute.

The search for purpose can be complicated by the existence of a hierarchy of purposes, that is, purposes that operate at different levels of generality with each higher level embracing more cases within its reach. This problem exists in all cases. Any statute has the general purpose of "doing good." Although a general purpose to "do good" may not seem to be a great deal of help in deciding concrete cases, it can be of some value, for it is merely a special instance of the Golden Rule. As such, at times it can be helpful in pointing out to the court the correct path to follow.

Often, however, the hierarchy of purposes is more complicated. A dramatic example is the Civil Rights Act of 1866, 42 U.S.C.A. § 1981 *et seq.* That statute, passed shortly after the end of the Civil War, has been said at various times (with support in the legislative history for each position) to have any of the following purposes: to grant newly freed slaves certain property rights, to grant that class civil rights, to do the same for all blacks, to do the same for all citizens. Some of those purposes are arguably inconsistent—the case of affirmative action comes readily to mind—and the court obviously must take care when it applies the statute to think about how its decision will affect the congery of legislative goals.

The creation of competing purposes will at times be deliberate. In those cases the legislature says in effect, "do this without doing that." This is often clearly expressed in the statute. The Statute of Frauds provision of the Uniform Commercial Code, § 2–201, requires that all contracts for the sale of goods with a value greater than $500 must be in writing if a court is to enforce the sale. The purpose of the required writing is to prevent fraud and mistakes, and to deter hasty decisions. On the other hand, the $500 floor is imposed to avoid burdening small transactions. At other times inconsistent purposes can be more difficult to reconcile. Section 2 of the Sherman Act, 15 U.S.C.A. § 2, prohibits "monopoliz[ing]". That language could be read as making illegal all monopolies. The courts, however, have refrained from such an expansive reading and have construed the policy of § 2 so as not to override the statutory grants of monopoly under the patent or copyright laws. Judges have also recognized that the statutory goal of prevention of concentration of economic power can conflict with another perceived goal of the Sherman Act, economic efficiency. The imposition of overly rigorous standards on businesses under § 2, for example, might deter firms from expanding and from being aggressive in research and marketing. Hence, decisions under § 2 have recognized a need to accommodate competing statutory goals. Needless to say, this can be a most

difficult task, and litigation under § 2 has proven
to be complex. Given the task of reconciling concepts as sophisticated as power and efficiency, however, that complexity is inescapable.

§ 5.5   "Intent" and "Purpose"

Judges and commentators often use the terms
"intent" and "purpose" interchangeably when discussing statutory interpretation. In spite of that
intermingling of usage, the two words over the past
three decades have acquired fairly well-known definitions and are often so used in detailed discussions on interpretation. The "intent" of the legislature refers to a solution that at least some of its
members had in mind with respect to a specific
application of the statute; in other words, the
outcome legislators envisioned for the type of case
now at bar. Legislative "purpose," on the other
hand, is both a more general and more objective
concept than that of legislative intent, for it refers
to legislative goals that transcend a particular application. Expressed differently, intent and purpose exist on a continuum that stretches from
some legislators' proposed solution to a specific
problem to the general idea of doing good for
society; as a researcher moves down the line from
intent to purpose the statute's coverage becomes
progressively more general.

The best argument for seeking legislative intent
is a practical one. As Reed Dickerson (supra,
§ 5.1) has argued, if a legislator has anything in

mind when voting on a statute (other than a suggestion from the floor leader as to which way to vote) it is intent, a desire to control a specific problem that has arisen. To the extent that statutory interpretation represents an effort to be realistic, therefore, an inquiry into intent seems to achieve that goal more nearly than does a search for purpose.

That argument is a strong one; however, both practical and theoretical objections can be raised against the search for intent. First, it can be argued that the search for the intent of the legislature is a search for a fiction. "Intent", as such, can exist only in the minds of individual members of the legislature, not, as such, in the legislative body. Beyond that, the expression of intent, except in the case of the most extraordinary of statutes, is confined to a very few members of one or two key committees. Decision-making that focuses on intent, therefore, necessarily confers a good deal of power on those legislators, because it relies on their understanding of the problem. A counter-argument is available here, however, for reliance on the work of the committee and a few key legislators can also be seen as judicial recognition of the way the legislative process works in a legislature that is hard pressed for time and expertise.

Practical objections to the search for intent also can be made. First the courts have often misused the "search" for intent. That search has encompassed some of the most dubious uses of legislative history in judicial annals. Justice Jackson's comment in United States v. Public Utilities Commission (1953) (concurring), is highly appropriate: "I should concur in this result more readily if the Court could reach it by analysis of the statute instead of by psychoanalysis of Congress." In searching for intent, courts have relied on statements by obscure legislators, passing references in a committee report, or history manufactured in a hearing by those interested in the outcome of a particular problem but lacking the votes to see that the outcome they seek is formally enacted. No wonder that legislative intent has acquired a bad reputation! Further, this inclination to search for bits and pieces of evidence to support an interpretation infects attorneys, who write briefs and ransack the legislative history for any oddments supporting their position, without thought to the presentation of a coherent and structured argument. The search for intent can also be expensive because useful material can be found almost anywhere in the legislative history; in contrast, the search for purpose is generally less expensive because its focus is on context, something that usually can be determined fairly quickly.

A final objection to the search for intent is that it hinders adapting a statute to changing conditions. A legislator's consideration generally focuses on the problem of the moment. Purpose is a more flexible tool, one more adaptable to new situations (this is discussed in more detail in § 5.25). A judge who relies on intent, therefore, will find it more difficult to adapt a statute to a changing society, and the inability to do so will thwart the satisfaction of purposes that underlay the passage of the statute.

An illustration of the problems created by the search for intent occurred following the adoption of the Nineteenth Amendment, giving women the right to vote. In Commonwealth v. Welosky (1931), appellant claimed that his conviction was improper because women had been excluded from his jury array in violation of state law. In Massachusetts at the time of the case, jury lists were drawn up pursuant to a statute that provided, "A person qualified to vote [for state legislators] shall be liable to serve as a juror." Although the court recognized that the term "person" could encompass women, it determined that because only men were qualified to vote at the time the statute was adopted, the "intent" of the legislature when it adopted the statute was to limit jury eligibility to men.

A different result might have been reached had the court inquired not into intent, but into the purpose of the legislature in tying jury lists to voting lists. The reason, in all probability, was administrative. A voting list gives the jury commissioner an easily accessible roster of presumably reasonable and responsible persons. That purpose is indifferent to the sex of the voter, for its rationale is convenience. The court's inquiry into intent, on the other hand, ineluctably reached the

conclusion that women should be excluded from
jury lists; the statute, after all, went to a time
when women did not have the vote, and the idea of
admitting women to the franchise was beyond the
frame of reference of the legislators, and, therefore, not within their intent. *Welosky* shows that
it can make a good deal of difference whether a
court's theory of interpretation leads it to search
for intent or for purpose.

It should not be thought from this that a search
for intent is without significance. In the first
place, intent can be helpful in showing statutory
purpose. A reader can often infer purpose from
specific examples in the legislative history by developing a rationale that explains why the legislature thought those results desirable and called for
by the statute. Further, that search is one that a
good lawyer cannot ignore, for whatever the validity of the objections to the use of legislative intent
in interpreting statutes, courts continually seek
such evidence. The reason is simple: judges look
for support wherever they can. Whether they
actually rely on what others have said or are
simply padding the record is immaterial; courts
make use of legislative intent in their opinions and
lawyers must be aware of that proclivity.

To sum up, both the judge who looks for "intent"
and the one who looks for "purpose" go back to the
enacting legislature to determine meaning. But
the judge searching for the former will inquire into
what the legislature actually would have done with

the problem before it, while the judge focusing on purpose will ask instead how the goal identified by that legislation can be achieved given the problem that is now before the court.

The vast majority of opinions today reflect a search either for intent or purpose (or often both). That search has not been without its critics, perhaps the most prominent of whom have been law and economics scholars led by Judges Easterbrook and Posner. A major complaint has been that traditional methods of statutory interpretation have ignored the realities of the legislative process, an area where interest groups and vote-trading often predominate.

§ 5.6   The Plain Meaning Rule

One more approach to questions of interpretation needs to be examined. Although it focuses less on how to interpret and more on what evidence can be used to do so, it is useful to discuss it here.

A curious hybrid of the literal and purposive approaches, the Plain Meaning Rule provides that sources other than the statute are not to be consulted unless the language of the statute is ambiguous; if the language is "plain" (i.e., not ambiguous) outside evidence bearing on interpretation cannot be admitted. The classic expression of the "Plain Meaning Rule" is found in Caminetti v. United States (1917): "Where the language is plain and admits of no more than one meaning the duty of interpretation does not arise and the rules which are to aid doubtful meanings need no discussion."

The Plain Meaning Rule does not purport to exclude all evidence of legislative purpose, or even to suggest that purpose is not the key to statutory interpretation. Instead, it merely *limits* the evidence available on the subject.* The Rule apparently grew out of recognition that neither the literal approach nor Golden Rule worked very well, a recognition that was coupled with distrust of the legislature and uncertainty with respect to the proper method of handling materials relating to legislative history. Gradually, however, courts came to place more trust in both the legislature and in their own handling of legislative history.

The Rule has also been subjected to a half century or more of judicial and scholarly criticism. Many of the same difficulties with the Golden Rule and the literal approach can be found with the Plain Meaning Rule. The major difficulty, of course, is determining when language is "plain". How can a court answer that question without examining all of the evidence that can be brought to bear? And what time frame is relevant to ascertain the "plainness" of meaning: the present,

---

* In this sense, the Plain Meaning Rule resembles another interpretive "rule", the parol evidence rule; the latter generally excludes extrinsic evidence of the meaning of a contract unless the language of the contract is "ambiguous". The parol evidence rule has also caused confusion and injustice and been the subject of much scholarly criticism. The parol evidence rule has been weakened in recent years.

when the event that caused the present litigation occurred, or when the statute was passed? By-passing these questions may make the judge's job easier, but they do not make judicial performance better.

All of this suggests, of course, that the Rule should be discarded. Ostensibly, however, it lives, and is frequently invoked even today. This may perhaps be done more out of custom than belief in its validity, for courts will quote the "Rule", find it applies, and still go on to look at extrinsic evidence. In United States v. Second Nat. Bank (1974), for example, the court went to some length to examine the "Plain Meaning Rule," and then proceeded to justify its result by an extended discussion of legislative history. A similar opinion from a state court is Baltimore Gas & Elec. Co. v. Board of County Commissioners (1976), in which the court professed it "unnecessary to look elsewhere" because the statute was "plain", and then proceeded to marshal further evidence to support its conclusion. In part, such mentions of the Rule merely reflect training and precedent; the judge may pay *pro forma* obeisance to the Rule before proceeding to "interpret" the statute.

"Magic words" (see § 4.7) may be harmless, but they may also be taken seriously and lead to serious error in the outcome of the case. Consider Caminetti v. United States (1917). There a man had transported his mistress from California to Nevada; the legal question was whether he could be convicted under the Mann Act, which made it illegal to take a woman across a state line for purposes of "prostitution, debauchery, or any other immoral purpose." Caminetti's conviction was upheld, the majority of the court finding that the language "or any other immoral purpose" was "plain" enough to cover his conduct. A vigorous dissent pointed to the legislative history to show that the purpose of the Act was (clearly) to prevent interstate commercialized vice, a purpose that would not be furthered by upholding the conviction. Invocation of the Plain Meaning Rule resulted in serious error.

Another example of problems created by the search for "plain meaning" can be found in Train v. Colorado Pub. Interest Research Group (1976). That case involved a requirement of the Federal Water Pollution Control Act that a permit be obtained before a "pollutant" could be discharged into navigable waters. The Act, 33 U.S.C.A. § 1362(6), defined "pollutant" to include such waste as "dredged spoil", "sewage", garbage", "discarded equipment", and "radioactive materials". The question the Supreme Court had to resolve was whether the statute applied to "radioactive materials" that were subject to regulation by the Atomic Energy Commission. The Court of Appeals held that it did, and in the process invoked the Plain Meaning Rule. In so holding, the court ignored substantial legislative history indicating that Congress had not contemplated requiring a permit for radioactive materials regulated by the

AEC. The Supreme Court reversed. Justice Marshall, speaking for an unanimous Court, and partially quoting from a 1940 decision, noted that:

> To the extent that the Court of Appeals excluded reference to the legislative history of the [Act] in discerning its meaning, the court was in error. As we have noted before: "When aid to construction of the meaning of words, as used in the statute, is available, there certainly can be no 'rule of law' which forbids its use, however clear the words may appear on 'superficial examination.' "

Turning for help to the legislative history, Justice Marshall held that the Act did not apply to "radioactive materials" regulated by the AEC.

The late 1980s, however, saw an unexpected revival of the plain meaning rule. Although there had been some earlier intimations of what was to come, the key event was the elevation to the Supreme Court of Justice Scalia. He immediately began a major assault on the use of committee reports, legislative history, and other external aids to fathom legislative intent. In a concurring opinion in INS v. Cardoza-Fonseca (1987), for example, he wrote: "Judges interpret laws rather than reconstruct legislators' intentions. Where the language of those laws is clear, we are not free to replace it with an unenacted legislative intent." And in United States v. Ron Pair Enterprises, Inc. (1989), the Court, in an opinion by Justice Blackmun, made clear that the Plain Meaning Rule would play a prominent role in the Court's decision-making: "The language before us expresses Congress' intent * * * with sufficient precision so that reference to legislative history and to pre-Code practice is hardly necessary."

The rebirth of plain meaning doctrine generally has been led by conservative jurists like Scalia. Their motivation does not appear to be ideological—to limit the scope of legislation passed by liberal Congresses. Rather, they seem to be influenced at least in part by dismay over the ridiculous uses sometimes made of legislative history, but more particularly out of concern that relying on the statutory history rather than on its text distorts the constitutional process. When legislative history controls the result, in other words, the prescribed method of enacting laws—passage by both Houses and signature by the President—is being ignored. See Eskridge, The New Textualism, 37 UCLA L.Rev. 621 (1990). As Scalia wrote in a concurring opinion: "[W]e have an obligation to conduct our exegesis in a fashion which fosters that democratic process." United States v. Taylor (1987).

That concern is well-placed; treating the history itself as *binding* does ignore proper constitutional procedures. Nevertheless, if the goal of statutory interpretation is to carry out legislative purpose, then there is nothing wrong with using the history of a statute's adoption to learn context, goals, purpose. Indeed, not to do so could well deny to legislation its proper scope and thereby deny Congress the full use of its constitutional power.

PART B
UNDERSTANDING THE STATUTE

Partial Summary. The *Nutshell* has taken the position that the duty of the courts in interpreting a statute is to recognize legislative supremacy in the area. Because legislators pass statutes to achieve certain ends, courts should try to ascertain the purpose of the statute and to implement that purpose in construing the statute in a case. The next several sections of this chapter deal more specifically with various methods by which the courts apprise themselves of legislative purpose.

§ 5.7 Internal Aids

All theories of interpretation recognize the importance of using internal evidence in statutory construction.

The statute's preamble often gives sound advice as to the purpose of the statute. Other operative sections of the statute can be very useful; for example, there may be a definition section, or perhaps uncertainty in one section can be cleared up in light of the purpose manifested in other parts of the act. Other statutes may be incorporated by reference; most legislatures, for example, have passed "dictionary" statutes which generally define a term such as a "person" (e.g., does it apply to a corporation?) for use whenever any statute refers to a "person".

§ 5.8   External Aids: General

General agreement exists on the use of intrinsic aids; less agreement exists on the use of extrinsic aids (those not found within the language of the statute). A few devices, however, provoke little or no controversy. The use of a dictionary, or perhaps a scientific manual to explain technical terms, falls within this category. Perhaps more attention should be paid here, however; we might well ask, for example, whether the use of a dictionary current at the time of the enactment is preferable to the use of a dictionary current at the time of the lawsuit.

The most commonly used extrinsic evidence is legislative history. The next several sections discuss its use in detail.

§ 5.9   Legislative History: General

Today American courts make widespread use of legislative history when interpreting statutes. Acceptance of such material, however, has not been without opposition. The next three sections discuss, first, arguments against the use of legislative history; next there is a discussion of specific types of legislative material; and, finally, a suggested approach to the consideration of legislative history.

§ 5.10 Drawbacks to Legislative History

Although there is little doubt that legislative history can be useful, widespread opposition to its use still can be found. There appear to be three bases for that opposition: unavailability, cost, and misuse.

a. *Availability*

In United States v. Public Utilities Commission of Calif. (1953), Justice Jackson, dissenting, strongly criticized judicial reliance on "inaccessible" legislative history, pointing to the difficulty counsel in that case had experienced in obtaining the relevant material. The history of a federal statute is more widely available than Justice Jackson suggested. Depositary libraries contain selected legislative material. In addition, most states have at least one regional library that receives a complete set of such materials. In addition to the libraries, specialized reporters, treatises, and other sources make legislative history available in particular areas. It is not at all difficult, for example, for a tax practitioner to find all relevant legislative history of a provision of the Internal Revenue Code; and the history of a major new statute is often readily available before the effective date of the act. Moreover, much of this is easily available on computer. Thus, inaccessibility, the problem pointed to by Jackson, is perhaps no longer as serious as he described.

The situation with respect to state statutes is less happy. Some states have no general published legislative history at all. In others availability is limited. In part this may have resulted from judicial reluctance to use history in interpretation, hindering development of a market for the material. In some states, perhaps most, the potential market is too slim to support publication and access to legislative history. Assuming that such material as committee reports is available in the legislative archives, it is still unavailable in practical terms to all but the most well-heeled planner or litigant. A court in such a state may well agree with Justice Jackson that it would be unfair to use that history. Several responses can be made to that argument. In the first place, the well-heeled will still use, both in planning and in litigation, what is available; judicial abstention simply renders that usage less effective. At the same time such abstention leads to a diminished quality of decision-making, an effect that has an impact on all citizens of the state, well-heeled or not. Alternatively, courts will use the history without admitting doing so; in that event the correctness of the use will not have been informed by the adversarial process.

Those counter-arguments have a good deal of validity. But it must be remembered that party expectations are based, necessarily, on reasonably available interpretive aids. Hence, a court must be careful to avoid using material not generally

available so as not to surprise unfairly those before
it.

b. Costs

Another objection to the use of legislative history
in interpretation is its cost. Rummaging among
lengthy volumes of hearing and testimony can be
time-consuming, tedious, and expensive. History
is at least relatively inaccessible and it can be very
difficult to digest. Is cost, however, an adequate
reason to issue decisions not as fully informed as
possible? Analogy might be drawn to other expensive but quite helpful aids to legal understanding:
law reviews, computer-assisted research, even the
basic library, all cost a great deal. As with legislative history, proper use of each of those sources
requires a highly trained researcher. Yet no one
suggests that those sources should be forbidden
fruit in the quest for understanding. Further, long
and complex legislative history would seem most
likely to be found in connection with important
statutes that attracted a good deal of attention; if
the legislature has devoted a great deal of effort to
solving a problem it would seem the courts should
investigate fully the fruits of that effort. Finally,
extreme cost would seem to be more closely associated with a search for intent rather than purpose,
for the former requires a careful and detailed look
at the whole process in order to find the legislative
"solution" to a situation not expressly covered by
the language of the statute; a search for purpose,

on the other hand, often need not be so complex because the aim is understanding legislative goals, a less tedious task.

c. Misuse

Judges and commentators alike have long commented on the opportunity for misusing legislative history. In using it courts often make no pretense that they have developed and are using a theory; instead, history often seems to be used selectively—referred to only when supportive of a conclusion arrived at by other means. Even when a court takes a more principled approach (one that it is willing to use in all similar cases), its methodology is often dubious. An example, discussed in § 5.21, is reliance on legislative failure to overturn a judicial interpretation of a statute. Perhaps the nadir of judicial failure to develop a well thought out approach to the use of legislative history is found in the Court's opinion in Citizens to Preserve Overton Park, Inc. v. Volpe (1971): "The legislative history is ambiguous * * *. Because of this ambiguity, it is clear that we must look primarily to the statutes themselves to find the legislative intent." That statement seems to stand the whole process on its head.

Misuse, however, should not lead to judicial renunciation of what can be a very effective tool. The real challenge is to develop—and adhere to—a method for dealing with legislative history.

d. A Final Word

Significant problems must be faced when deciding whether to open the door for consideration of legislative history. The British have resolutely refused to take that path; the classic statement on that attitude comes from Assam Rys. and Trading Co., Ltd. v. Inland Rev. Comm'rs. (1935) where the House of Lords refused to consider a Royal Commission report offered to show Parliamentary intention:

> [T]he intention of the legislature must be ascertained from the words of the statute with such extraneous assistance as is legitimate. * * * It is clear that the language of a minister of the Crown in proposing in Parliament a measure * * * is inadmissible and the report of Commissioners is even more removed from value as evidence of intention, because it does not follow that their recommendations were accepted.

English courts are willing, however, to consider legislative materials if they bear on the circumstances that surround the passage of the bill rather than on the intention of Parliament. (It must be an arduous task to keep those two considerations well separated.)

In this country there seems to be no turning back from our embrace of legislative history. Our courts have concluded that the benefits of the practice far outweigh the drawbacks. There is good reason for that conclusion. As a member of the House of Lords said while disagreeing with his colleagues' view: "To refuse to consider such a commentary, when Parliament has legislated on the basis and faith of it, is for the interpreter to fail to put himself in the real position of the promulgator of the instrument before essaying its interpretation. It is refusing to follow what is perhaps the most important clue to meaning. It is perversely neglecting reality while chasing the shadows." Black–Clawson Intern. Ltd. v. Papierwerke Waldhof–Aschaffenburg A.G. (1975) (Lord Simon of Glaisdale, dissenting). Contributing to the intrinsic worth of the historical materials for American judges is the help they provide in easing relations with a co-ordinate branch of government. Practical persons, they seek help where they can find it. At the beginning of our history as a nation, Chief Justice Marshall voiced that view: "Where the mind labours to discover the design of the legislature, it seizes everything from which aid can be derived." United States v. Fisher (1804). There is, however, another side to the coin. Judges must be alert for the probative value of the material they consider. They must be careful to analyze that material in light of the rest of the statute, the surrounding circumstances, and the remainder of the *corpus juris*. Common sense and intellectual honesty, when employed by a knowledgeable court, can mint at least some gold from the ore of legislative history.

The next section explores the working of this legislative process. Then, in § 5.12, an approach to the use of legislative history is suggested.

§ 5.11 The Legislative Process

To understand the value of different types of legislative history it is necessary to understand the legislative process. This can be briefly sketched; for more detail see J. Davies, Legislative Law and Process in a Nutshell (2d ed. 1986).

A Bill Is Introduced. It may have originated in a message from the President (or Governor; the federal scheme is typical); it may be a project of a Senator, or it may have originated in an investigative hearing. In some states the bill may have been the product of a continuing law revision committee, or the report of a blue ribbon commission studying a problem. The bill is referred to a committee (or to a subcommittee), which holds hearings on it. Witnesses testify in the hearings, often on two (or more) sides of the issue. Their testimony can be written or oral; it may be argumentative or factual. Committee members or staff may cross-examine or not.

Following the hearing the committee votes on the bill. If the vote is favorable, it is reported out to, say, the Senate. The majority writes a report describing the bill, why it is thought desirable, and, perhaps, explaining some of the choices in drafting and in substance. The purpose of the report is both to persuade other legislators to vote for it and to explain the bill after it has been enacted. Opponents of the bill may issue a minority report, in an attempt to convince legislators to vote against the bill. Called up for action, the committee chair and the sponsor will explain the goals sought by the bill, and how it will achieve them. They will respond to questions and other Senators may also speak. If the Senate passes the bill, it will be referred to the House, where the process begins anew; this time, however, the Senate bill will be used as the starting point. (Sometimes similar bills will work their way through both houses more or less at the same time.) Hearings, committee report, debate, and vote follow in the same order as before.

If the Senate and House versions of the bill differ, a Joint Committee will try to iron out the differences. If it does, still another report called the Conference Report will issue. The bill is then sent back to give each House a chance to pass or defeat the work of the Joint Committee, creating still more legislative history.

It can be readily seen from this synopsis that a fair amount of legislative history can accrue during the process; controversial legislation such as the Civil Rights Act of 1964 can accumulate truly impressive volumes of material. The question for the lawyer and judge, of course, is—what do we do with it? Although a large part of the answer to that question depends on the relevant theory of interpretation, the answer also requires understanding of what goes on at key stages in the legislative process.

The Hearing. In theory, at least, the hearing provides Congress with much of the information needed to form the basis of its action. Testimony at the hearing is useful, therefore, as background information concerning the purpose of the statute—what problems did Congress perceive and what were its goals in addressing those problems? The hearings may show how a bill evolved, a process that can shed light on what the Congress was doing. Because the testimony often is not tested by effective cross-examination, it must be carefully evaluated before permitting it to have any effect. An extended hearing, for example, often provides material for almost any conceivable position, making the hearing into a process that often serves only to build a record; to manufacture, as the phrase goes, legislative history. This practice is well known, but judges at times seem oblivious to that fact as they rummage through testimony presented at hearings to find evidence to support a decision reached by other means.

The hearing also provides an opportunity for various sides to express a position on the problem and to make clear their "understanding" of what the bill does and does not do. Since those are partisan statements, they too must be carefully scrutinized. The understanding that "this bill is not intended to do X", on the other hand, when agreed to by opposite sides, becomes relatively non-partisan, presenting effective evidence of legislative understanding with respect to purpose.

The hearing, to sum up, can provide good background material that helps to place the statute in context. Material derived from the hearing must be used with great care, however, for it is very easy to read more into the record than it warrants. The use of material from hearings is also limited by the expense of doing so (mainly time consumed in perusing heavy volumes of transcripts) and its comparative unavailability.

Committee Report. The most useful of all legislative history, the report reflects the considered judgment (more or less) of those legislators most familiar with the problems addressed by the proposal, and their manner of solution. The committee report provides, in short, an excellent source of legislative purpose. Further, the report is far and away the most likely source of information to be consulted by the rest of Congress (if anything at all is consulted); hence, the intent of Congress (if that is your inquiry) can best be found in the report. A report from certain committees carries even greater weight because the rest of Congress defers to that body. The best example is the House Ways and Means Committee reports on tax legislation. The tax laws are highly complex and technical and it is natural for courts to place great weight on the reports of that committee. That reliance recognizes Congressional deference to Ways and Means along with the necessity of having a source that will help fit together the old and new laws. Doing so is of especial importance in the tax area due to the need of private parties to have reliable sources to help facilitate planning. A final advantage to committee reports is their relative availability.

In spite of those advantages the committee report is, in the end, only a memorandum drafted by a small group of legislators; the primary source of meaning must still be the language of the act itself, for that is the only legislative work adopted according to constitutional procedures. Further, the report may not be altogether reliable; proponents of the bill, for example, may minimize the change the bill will accomplish in the hope that it will not appear controversial and scare away potential supporters. A dissent to a committee report must be carefully viewed, for it is easy to over-state (or misstate) the impact of the bill in order to crystallize opposition to it. The dissent can be useful, however, to highlight problems in the language and goals of the statute.

The Conference Report may have a special status. Justice Frankfurter, dissenting in Commissioner v. Acker (1959), called the Conference Report "the most authoritative report"; because "acted upon by both Houses," it "unequivocally represents the will of both Houses."

Floor Debates. Statements made on the floor of a house should have little effect on interpretation. In the first place, debate, as such, rarely occurs. Discussion on the floor often consists of the committee chair or sponsor making a few remarks and then being fed a few questions by a friendly legislator in order to build a record for adjudication. The value of such statements is questionable, for failure to incorporate the material in the report suggests that such statements may not reflect the views of the majority of the committee (as the speaker sometimes concedes), as of course would be true if the response were to problems first noticed following the report. In any event, the precision of the report is lacking; words spoken extemporaneously may not convey quite the meaning the speaker wished. Lending force to that observation is the fact that a debate seeks to persuade; it does not necessarily seek to enlighten.

Statements from other speakers seem relatively useless except as they may shed some light on purpose. Most debates, after all, involve only a few members; even assuming the exchange of comments among them provides insight, extrapolation of that insight to the whole Congress is most problematic.

The Executive. The message accompanying legislation originating with the President can be very useful in defining statutory purpose. It is important to remember that legislation can change during the course of the legislative process, and an executive message has to be evaluated with that in mind. The executive, on the other hand, speaks for a coordinate branch of government and his voice should be accorded equivalent weight. The

President also seeks to achieve certain ends when he approves of legislation, ends that also should be given a constitutionally recognized place in its enactment.

§ 5.12 A Suggested Approach

The most important thing to remember when construing a statute is that the words of the statute are the primary device the legislature uses for conveying meaning. Because those words may not adequately convey to the court the goals sought by the legislature the context of the statute must also be examined. For that task it is appropriate to consider legislative history. In doing so, the court should consider both the evidentiary value of the proffered material and, secondarily, the availability of that material for use by others.

Consideration of the evidentiary value should be a familiar task to the court, for that is a constant inquiry it undertakes in many contexts. Here it is important to remember the manner in which the legislature operates. Generally, the committee and Conference reports have the most value, followed by certain statements in "debate", and last by material from hearings; the weight of an executive message can vary depending on changes in the proposed legislation. Each item of history must be further evaluated in the light of good sense. Good sense has two components: first, the court must evaluate the way that the material fits in the total picture painted by the adoption process of the statute at bar; next, it must consider how the material contributes to understanding what the legislature was doing.

Availability has importance in terms of expectations. Judicial reliance on materials that cannot be obtained by the general public may be deemed unfair if it upsets expectations based on more readily available material.

Finally, as Justice Frankfurter wrote, it matters "whether you start with an answer or with a problem." Some Reflections on the Readings of Statutes, 47 Colum.L.Rev. 527 (1947). Read the statute, ponder it, reflect on its purpose; reach a preliminary understanding of what the statute is about, how it fits with the rest of the law, where the problems are. Then turn to extrinsic evidence to help resolve any questions.

PART C
MORE ON UNDERSTANDING

The next part of this Chapter examines several methods that help the court understand the goals the legislature had in mind when it adopted the statute. They range from further consideration of context to the use of canons of construction.

§ 5.13 A Summary at Mid–Point

The legislature has the primary voice when it acts within the Constitution. The court's job, then, is to give effect to what the legislature has passed.

In doing so, the most important factor is the language of the statute, the manner in which the legislature expressed its desires. The touchstone of this process is purpose: the aim or goal of the statute. In understanding purpose the court must set the statute in context; context is found by looking at the circumstances that surrounded its passage. Useful in this process is legislative history, especially committee and conference reports. All material—extrinsic or intrinsic—must be checked for probative value. In addition, the availability of such materials may influence the use made of them. Reliance on them should not be restricted by theories such as the Plain Meaning Rule that artificially limit access to evidence that would help the court understand the statute. Finally, the court's obligation to engage in principled and consistent decision making does not cease because it is dealing with statutes.

§ 5.14   Context: Reenactment

Throughout this Chapter the importance of evaluating a statute in context has been emphasized. Thus, courts recognize the importance of context when several statutes operate in the same area; in that situation judges strive to harmonize statutes with one another, to find a reading that minimizes the disruption of the goals sought by each.

A related phenomenon occurs with the passage of a bill that amends an existing statute. A court in applying the amendment must focus on the legislature's purpose in changing the law; at the same time the court must be careful to recognize that patterns of behavior have grown up around the old law, patterns that should not be disturbed unless necessary to achieve the goals of the new law. To put it differently, conduct is influenced by expectations formed by those affected by the statute over the period that the statute has been in existence. The legislature, of course, can change those expectations, but the signal to do so should be clear enough so that all who are affected can understand the force of what has been done. (The effect of *stare decisis* in interpretation is discussed in § 5.24.) This is a most important consideration when construing a statute that has been reenacted; hence, failure of those who have an interest in doing so to modify their behavior should be considered by a court in construing the effect of the amendment. Especially important is the need to insure that change in statutory language does not lead to accidental results.

It can be difficult of course to distinguish between those two poles. Especially helpful here is the context as shown by committee reports and legislative hearings; scholarly and practical commentary following the amendments can help show what the purpose and effect of the amending process was popularly understood to be. An example can be found in Edmonds v. Compagnie Generale Transatlantique (1979), involving the 1972 Amendments to the Longshoremen's and Harbor Workers' Act. The Court of Appeals in that case had found that the amendments had modified a longshore-man's rights against a vessel. The Supreme Court rejected that view. After noting that the legislative history did not mention such a change, the Court said: "This silence is most eloquent, for such reticence while contemplating an important and controversial change is unlikely."

Another form of this problem occurs when the legislature codifies or recodifies the law in an area. There is a strong presumption that such changes do not disturb previous interpretations of the statute. Two good reasons support that presumption. First, the purpose of codification is not substantive. Its goal, rather, is to make statutory law more coherent by systematizing the location of the acts, correcting typographical errors, and so forth. Those purposes are non-controversial; if, however, they were to have a substantive impact the changes might become controversial and the codification difficult to clear with the legislature. Hence the legislative purpose is merely to clear up certain problems. For the court to read substantive change into the process would be to create a purpose that was not there.

The presumption that codification does not change existing law can lead to interesting problems if the codification committee does not perform its job properly. Because interpretation does not change there may be a gap between "law", as reflected in prior cases and commentary, and the new words of the statute. Thus, codification has the potential for making a lawyer's job harder rather than easier. Codifiers have to be very careful to avoid that problem.

§ 5.15 Legislative Control of Interpretation

Legislatures occasionally pass interpretive acts, statutes designed to guide courts in determining the meaning of other statutes. The existence of a Uniform Statutory Construction Act, and the adoption of that or a similar act in a number of states suggests the need felt by legislatures to try and control its product after a statute has left the state house. The history of interpretive acts has shown them generally to be innocuous. Occasionally, however, a suggestion has been made that such statutes are unconstitutional.

A provision of the Illinois Antitrust Act, for example, stated that the courts were to construe that Act in the same way that the Federal courts construed the federal antitrust laws. A section in the Illinois Constitution, however, provided that no branch of the government shall exercise powers belonging to another, and that the legislative, executive and judicial branches were separate. The Illinois Supreme Court held that because the judicial power was vested solely in the courts, the legislature was without power to state explicitly how the judiciary was to construe a statute. People v. Crawford Distributing Co. (1972).

A different experience with interpretation statutes is illustrated by the Pennsylvania Statutory

Construction Act. Most of the Act's provisions are non-controversial and are directed at future legislatures rather than at the courts. There are, however, three sections prescribing interpretive rules, defining terms, and setting out canons of construction for the court to follow. Most of the provisions are banal; a notable exception is a section providing that the doctrine that statutes in derogation of the common law will be strictly construed will have no application when the court interprets statutes passed after enactment of the Act.

One study of the Pennsylvania Act found that it was used in fewer than 3% of the cases where the court construed statutes. Comment, The Effect of the Statutory Construction Act in Pennsylvania, 12 Univ. of Pitt.L.Rev. 283 (1951). Of course, in some cases the court may have followed the Act without specifically alluding to it. In almost every case where the "anti-derogation" section discussed above was cited, however, the court applied the strict construction canon despite the contrary provision of the Act. This was done shortly after the passage of the Act, for example, in Null v. Staiger (1939).

In short, the legislature can attempt to impose guidelines on the courts for the interpretation of statutes, but it cannot compel a court to follow them. Courts may consider these Acts to be merely advisory. Obviously, interpretive acts are themselves subject to interpretation by the courts.

§ 5.16   The Role of Fundamental Values

The preceding chapter (see § 4.23), referred to the role played by fundamental values in common law decision making. Basic values play a role in statutory interpretation as well. The core idea is the same in both areas: The law maker should not be casually thought, absent good evidence to the contrary, to have made a law that disregards those principles. This "policy of clear statement", as Hart and Sacks (supra, § 4.2 at 1240) call it, recognizes that the legislature, as well as the court, operates within the context of our whole jurisprudence—and some threads of that are stronger than others.

A good deal of case law supports this proposition. An example is Santa Clara Pueblo v. Martinez (1978), in which the Court was asked to imply a private cause of action under the Indian Civil Rights Act of 1968, 25 U.S.C.A. § 1302(8). The Court refused to do so, despite the fact that the statutory language was such that normally a cause of action would be implied. The refusal was based, a later Court noted, on a long held "special policy against judicial interference" in Indian affairs. Cannon v. University of Chicago (1979).

Courts consult a number of sources to ascertain fundamental values; the policy against interference in Indian affairs, for example, can be found in statutes and judicial decisions. The Constitution also represents a source of values which, if not controlling, at least inform a court with respect to values normally associated with legislation by implication. Two famous cases involve the construction of statutes in the light of our national attitude toward religion. The first, Girouard v. United States (1946), posed the question whether an alien who had refused to serve in the Armed Forces on the ground that he was a conscientious objector could be naturalized. In holding for the alien the court referred to our nation's long tradition of religious freedom. As Justice Douglas commented: "We do not believe that Congress intended to reverse that policy when it came to draft the naturalization oath. Such an abrupt and radical departure from our traditions should not be implied."

Similarly, in Holy Trinity Church v. United States (1892), the Court relied on the observation that "no purpose of action against religion can be imputed to any *legislation,* State or Nation, because this is a religious people." The statute there in question forbade anyone to assist in the immigration of aliens "to perform labor or services of any kind." The government had invoked that statute against a church that had hired an English clergyman. The Court held that the statute did not apply despite its apparently clear language. After inquiring into the purpose of the statute—to protect the nation against "an ignorant and servile class"—it noted that "labor" should be read to include manual labor. "But beyond that," Justice Brewer argued, "the statute must be read against our religious tradition," a tradition whose existence he went to some length to demonstrate. Hence, the Court held, the Congress could not have had the "intentions" of making illegal the contract with a clergyman.

Legislation should also be interpreted in the light of values drawn from the common law. Judicial decisions, too, reflect the values of our society and can be drawn upon to help us understand legislation. In Glus v. Brooklyn Eastern Dist. Terminal (1959), for example, plaintiff asserted that a three year statute of limitation did not bar a cause of action because the actions of the defendant estopped it from raising the defense. Although the statute did not mention estoppel, the court had no trouble with the case. Invoking the maxim that "no man may take advantage of his own wrong", a "principle of law older than the country itself," the court held for the plaintiff.

That maxim was also employed in Riggs v. Palmer (1889). Elmer Palmer claimed property of his grandfather's under a will. Although there was no question that the will left the property to Elmer, there was a catch—Elmer had murdered his grandfather, apparently to prevent him from changing his will. In New York, the passing of property at death is regulated extensively by a number of statutes which, as the court pointed out, "if literally construed * * * give this property to the murderer."

The court found that result difficult to accept. In holding against Elmer, it noted first that the legislature could never have had the "intention" of permitting a murderer to profit from his wrong in this way, and then,

> that a thing which is within the intention of the makers of a statute is as much within the statute as if it were within the letter; and a thing which is within the letter of the statute is not within the statute unless it be within the intention of the makers.

The court then justified its belief that the legislature could not have intended this result by referring to the civil law, and to cases denying recovery to a beneficiary under a life insurance contract who had murdered the insured. Finally, the court explained that the statutes relating to passage of property at death did not address the question at bar because "[i]t was evidently supposed that the maxims of the common law were sufficient to regulate such a case and that a specific enactment for the purpose was not needed."

Although other courts have disagreed strongly, the approach in Riggs v. Palmer seems correct. A legislature acts against the backdrop of the common law. It expects a court to carry out as fully as possible the policies adopted in the statutes; on the other hand, because it is addressing general problems, not all details of application can be solved in the act itself. When a court fills in those details, it may reasonably suppose that the legislature has said, in effect: "Look, carry out our purpose, but recognize that that purpose does not include unnec-

essary interference with other areas of the law. It
is up to you, courts, to adjust the balance."

That reading of legislation is another way of
saying that a statute should be construed *in pari
materia* not only with other statutes, but with the
common law as well. Doing so is similar to the
process used when the common law itself changes
(see the discussion of the right of privacy in § 4.18);
in both cases the principle limiting the new development is the need to disrupt existing law as little
as possible.

§ 5.17   Canons of Construction

Over the centuries courts and commentators developed a number of catch-phrases to express common approaches to problems of interpretation.
Those maxims contain common sense. When used
properly by a court they can help suggest, both to
the court and to others who work with a statute
what the legislature had in mind when it drafted a
statute. Unfortunately, many courts have given
more weight to canons of construction than they
can properly bear, often writing opinions as if a
particular canon controlled—by its own force—disposition of the case at bar. Attribution of that
kind of force to what is nothing more than a
specialized proverb is a risky business. Like a
proverb, each canon has a "counter-canon" running the opposite way. (Karl Llewellyn compiled a
glorious list of the "Thrust" and "Parry" of "Canons of Construction" in his Remarks on the Theory

of Appellate Decision and the Rules or Canons About How Statutes are to be Construed, 3 Vand.L. Rev. 395 (1950)). Selection of the canon to be used, therefore, is the key step in any interpretive process that relies on their use. The canons, however, give no clues as to when each should be properly invoked. Thus, their use in decision-making obscures the key step in the process.

That criticism suggests a more fundamental problem with decision-making by key phrases. Statutory interpretation is too complex to leave to a single word or phrase. This is not to suggest, however, that canons are useless. Handled carefully they have a place in the judge's craft-bag. Although not a substitute for analysis, they can suggest possible ways to interpret a statute properly.

A number of common canons are discussed in the following sections. The remainder of this section addresses several canons dealing with meaning; the next two sections focus on commonly invoked maxims that take the form of presumptions.

a. *Noscitur a Sociis,* or, "words take meaning from those with which they are associated." This maxim reflects the need to evaluate language in the context in which it is used. An application of the maxim can be seen in Dunham v. State (1939), in which the court upset defendant's conviction for converting money entrusted to him for investment in the stock market. The statute under which he had been convicted made it a crime for a "factor, commission merchant, warehouse keeper * * * stage driver, or other common carrier * * * or any other person with whom any property * * * may be entrusted or deposited * * *'" to "fraudulently convert" money entrusted to him. The court reasoned that because the occupations specified in the statute were "governed by the law of bailments", the "broader term 'any other person' was meant to refer to one following a like pursuit." Because defendant's activity was not subject to the law of bailment, he could not be convicted under the statute.

b. *Ejusdem Generis*

A general term that follows a set of specific terms is to be limited to items of the same general class as contained in the recital of specifics. A limited version of *noscitur a sociis,* the idea behind this maxim is that the draftsmen listed specific illustrations and then inserted a catch-all phrase to insure coverage of all items. An illustration is 18 U.S.C.A. § 1462 which prohibits the importation into the United States of "[a]ny obscene, lewd, lascivious, or filthy book, pamphlet, picture, motion-picture film, paper, letter, writing, print, or other matter of indecent character * * *." Here, the general class of "indecent" matter is partially defined by the listing of "book, pamphlet, picture", etc.

The major difficulty in applying *ejusdem generis* inheres in the difficulty in determining the scope of the general class.   In Cleveland v. United States (1946), petitioners had been convicted of violating the Mann Act, 18 U.S.C.A. § 398, which prohibits the transportation in interstate commerce of "any woman or girl for the purpose of prostitution or debauchery or for any other immoral purpose." Petitioner, a practitioner of polygamy based on religious beliefs, had transported one of his wives across a state line.   Because that conduct did not fill the proscriptions against "prostitution" nor "debauchery" the case turned on whether polygamy was an "immoral purpose."

Both sides in the Supreme Court applied the *ejusdem generis* rule, the majority concluding that polygamy, being illegal activity with "sexual connotations," was "immoral."   Dissenting, Justice Murphy argued that the terms "prostitution" and "debauchery" established a more narrow class, dealing with commercialized vice.   Hence, the freedom of the petitioners in *Cleveland* turned on the definition of a class established by *ejusdem generis*.

c.   *Expressio Unius Est Exclusio Alterius*

"The expression of some excludes others."   An example is Fazio v. Pittsburgh Ry. Co. (1936). There, a statute stated that "every allegation of fact" in a complaint was deemed to be admitted if it had not been denied.   Another section of the act, however, listed several specific types of allegations which, if not denied, were to be taken as admitted. The court ruled the enumeration of specific items excluded the application of the general language of the statute to allegations other than those that the legislature had enumerated. In short, the *expressio unius* maxim, like the other maxims mentioned so far, suggests that the legislature was trying to achieve a *limited* goal when it passed the law, and the limits were expressed in the language used.

d. Terms of Art

Words that bear a specific meaning to a class at whom a statute is directed are construed the way that class would do so. Such terms of art can be technical, legal, or commercial. A court interpreting a statute referring, for example, to the "indestructibility of contingent remainders" (one of the more esoteric areas of the law of future interests), will give that term its technical legal meaning. A statute referring to a technical accounting term such as "surplus" will be read the way an accountant would read it. Although the interpretation of terms of art presents no theoretical problem, there are two practical problems of which a court should be wary. It must be sure that a term was used in its technical sense, and it must be careful that it has correctly ascertained a meaning associated with an unfamiliar technical term.

Sometimes a statute carries its own dictionary in the form of a list of definitions provided by the legislature. This represents a specialized version of the term of art rule; in those statutes the "art" the "term" refers to is the statute itself.

§ 5.18 Statutes in Derogation of the Common Law

One very old canon tells us that statutes that change the common law are to be construed strictly. Some have explained the canon as a manifestation of judicial hostility toward legislation. Certainly there is support for that position. American law at the turn of the present century was in the heyday of strict construction of statutes. Judges of that period were often more conservative than legislators and often invoked the maxim in connection with progressive social legislation. An example is Jones v. Milwaukee Elec. Ry. & Light Co. (1911). There, a statute imposing employer's liability on "every railroad company" was held not to apply to an "electric interurban railroad company." Such hostility, of course, is improper in that it denies proper scope to legislative desires. Limitation of legislation due to hostility, in other words, manifests judicial supremacy in an area—law making—where the legislature should be supreme.

One attempt to justify the maxim centers on a "presumption" that the Legislature acted with full knowledge of the canon of strict construction. That presumption is a remarkable one. Not only does it suffer from the other problems that arise when legislation is interpreted so as to conform with judicial notions of what the legislature should do (see § 5.22), but the presumption is contrary to fact. Consider a legislature that is in the process of enacting legislation that has been the subject of extensive hearings and has been agonized over, subjected to compromise, etc: Is it likely that a responsible member of that legislature would also attach a rider that says, in effect, "construe all ambiguities against this statute, do not extend it to implement fully its purpose, and do not use it as a basis for analogical reasoning"? That does not appear to be a plausible scenario.

It may be possible, however, to justify—partially—the strict construction canon. This justification is based on legislative recognition of the need to fit any new law into the framework of the existing *corpus juris* ("body of law"). Hence, although a court must construe a statute so as to carry out its purpose fully, at the same time, the court must harmonize the act with the surrounding common law landscape. Adjustment of the tension between those demands may require a good deal of careful brush work; again, the judge works as artist as well as architect.

§ 5.19   Strict Construction of Penal Statutes

One of the most commonly invoked maxims of construction tells us that penal statutes should be strictly construed. On first impression, that stricture appears to make sense. Primarily it reflects a policy of fairness; someone should not be held criminally accountable for conduct that she could not reasonably know was illegal.

So fundamental is the belief in fairness that it has secured partial Constitutional recognition (in cases where the statute is overly vague). In Lanzetta v. New Jersey (1939), the Supreme Court ruled that a statute that made it a crime to be a member of a "gang" violated the due process clause of the Fourteenth Amendment; the term "gang" was so vague as not to put possible violators of the act fairly on notice concerning their exposure to criminal sanctions.

The void-for-vagueness doctrine, however, does not invalidate all less than "clear" statutes. As Jerome Hall noted in General Principles of Criminal Law (2d ed. 1960), it is important to separate the case of a statute that is ambiguous from that which is vague. In the case of an ambiguous statute a person need not guess at what conduct is permissible, but can conform his conduct so as to comply with the possible meanings. That is especially true where the conduct in question is generally believed to be illegal or immoral. In those cases there is little reason to construe a penal statute differently than a civil one. There are many cases where the court invokes the strict construction maxim, sometimes applying it with a vengeance. Insuring fair warning to a defendant is a laudable goal, but so is proper implementation of legislative directives.

Viewed in that fashion the construction of a penal statute does not vary significantly from application of crimes defined at common law to a particular case. Indeed, although today most "common law" crimes have been codified, the statutory definitions are typically imprecise and rely on general statements to define wrongful conduct. Still, those statutes have not run into "strict construction" difficulties, even though no one pretends that an ordinary criminal (or even a law student) could analyze the case law to differentiate between, say, larceny by trick and false pretenses (even though that might be the difference between a felony and a misdemeanor.) The reason for the comparative lack of concern with respect to common law crimes can be traced to the fact the common law does represent community values, and the defendant, although perhaps not exactly sure of what crime has been committed, has been amply warned of its wrongfulness. Finally, both common law and statutory crimes cannot be used freely by a prosecutor to "go after" anyone she dislikes, for in both cases the prosecutor is limited by the definitions of the crime found either in case law or statute.

The most famous American case is McBoyle v. United States (1931). McBoyle had been convicted of violating a federal statute that made it illegal to transport a "motor vehicle," known to have been stolen, across a state line. (The "motor vehicle" in the case was an airplane.) "Motor vehicle" was defined as "an automobile, automobile truck, auto-

mobile wagon, motor cycle, or any other self-pro-
pelled vehicle not designed for running on rails."
The Supreme Court set aside the conviction. Writing for a unanimous Court, Justice Holmes noted
that the definition of motor vehicle "indicates that
a vehicle in the popular sense, that is a vehicle
running on land, is the theme." He then added:
"It is reasonable that a fair warning should be
given to the world in language that the common
world will understand * * *."

The court did not directly address the question of
whether McBoyle's conviction fell within the pur-
view of the Act. That would seem a better place to
begin analysis of the problem; once it is decided
whether the Act applies, the court can focus specifically on the fair warning problem. Breaking
down the analysis in this two-step fashion carries
with it the advantage of directing attention to the
two completely different issues involved: Is this
the type of situation the statute was designed to
reach, and is it "fair" to do so in the case at bar?
Collapsing the two lines of inquiry, as *McBoyle* did,
may confuse the analysis.

McBoyle's transportation across a state line of
an aircraft he knew to have been stolen seems to
have been within the range of conduct Congress
sought to reach—presumably to aid local police in
the very difficult task (for local police) of stopping
interstate crime. Indeed, the problem is more
acute with airplanes, given the ease and quickness
with which state lines can be crossed. Finally, the

language of the act—"vehicle"—certainly can include an airplane. (Holmes also found significant the fact that the statute was passed in 1919, a time when Congress "knew" of airplanes, but did not mention them directly; the silence was perhaps due to the fact that the problem of stolen aircraft was not significant at that time).

Now what of the fair warning problem? McBoyle certainly knew that his conduct was illegal. He was transporting an item he knew to be stolen. That is a commonly recognized crime. It is exceedingly unlikely (as Holmes recognized) that McBoyle would consult the statute before acting; even if he had, he should have been aware that his conduct *might* violate federal law. Since it did violate local law he had ample advance notice of the possible consequences of his actions. Further, McBoyle, unlike the "gangsters" in *Lanzetta,* should have had no trouble conforming his activity to the statute. If there was ambiguity or uncertainty as to the scope of the term "vehicle" it served to reinforce the deterrent effect of state criminal law. Consequently, the doctrine of fair warning was not applicable in the case.

Routine application of the strict construction doctrine leads, as *McBoyle* suggests, to results that are difficult to defend. Hence, rejection of the doctrine can be found in a number of cases. In United States v. Shirey (1959), for example, Justice Frankfurter wrote (partially quoting an earlier case): "Statutes, including penal enactments, are not inert exercises in literary composition. They are instruments of government, and in construing them the general purpose is a more important aid to the meaning than any rule which grammar or formal logic may lay down." And in United States v. Brown (1948), the Court observed:

> The canon in favor of strict construction [of criminal statutes] is not an inexorable command to override common sense and evident statutory purpose * * *. Nor does it demand that a statute be given the "narrowest meaning"; it is satisfied if the words are given their fair meaning in accord with the manifest intent of the lawmakers.

Still, courts continue to cite the strict construction maxim when convenient. Generally, it appears not to play a significant role in the decision. See, e.g., Dunn v. United States (1979), where the Court invoked the maxim apparently as a makeweight to bolster an opinion decided through conventional statutory analysis. Often, however, the maxim is invoked only to cast it aside, or it is not mentioned at all. A court's approach to interpretation should be disciplined enough not to give the appearance of deliberate use of interpretive techniques only when convenient. Especially in this area it is important to instruct lower courts in the values recognized by the strict construction maxim, for it reminds us of a fundamental principle: that a legislature should not be thought to have mandated serious penalties unless the person to whom the statute has been addressed fairly knows that his conduct entails serious risks.

PART D
SUBSEQUENT DEVELOPMENTS

The construction of a statute can be significantly influenced by events that occur after the statute has been adopted. The ability of the legislature to control future problems is limited by the growth that accretes to the statute over the years. Expectations form based on the way the statute has been construed and a court must recognize their impact on the decision making process. This part of the Chapter on interpretation focuses on such questions.

§ 5.20 Post–Enactment Evidence of "Legislative History"

Courts pay little attention to statements made by legislators after a bill has been passed. A rare comment on the problem occurred in Alaska Pub. Employees Ass'n v. State (1974), in which an affidavit by a bill's "prime sponsor" had been submitted, stating what he and his committee had understood the bill to mean. The Alaska Supreme Court ruled that such affidavits "should not be considered by a court in construing legislative intent. We do not wish to transform statutory construction into a parade of legislators' affidavits containing their perception of the meaning of a bill." To allow the introduction of such evidence might be tempting in a state where legislative history is generally unavailable, but it is a course that should be avoided. As a British judge explained: "[I]n construing a statute I believe the worst person to construe it is the person responsible for its drafting. He is very much disposed to confuse what he intended to do with the effect of the language which in fact has been employed." Hilder v. Dexter (1902). And in Motor Vehicle Mfrs. Ass'n v. State Farm Mut. Auto. Ins. Co. (1983), the Court expressly rejected the notion that post-enactment statements by members of Congress could change the standard of review applicable to agency decision-making.

§ 5.21 Legislative Inaction

A variation on the reenactment problem discussed earlier (§ 5.14) arises when the legislature *fails* to act. A large body of case law has found significance in such inaction. The cases fall generally into two categories. First, some cases find significance in legislative failure to pass certain proposed bills, treating the failure to pass the bill as a kind of legislative *veto* over the course of action contained in the defeated proposal. Second, some cases view legislative inaction following judicial construction of a statute as similar to *acquiescence* by the legislature in that construction. Although those two situations present different problems, the analysis raises a common preliminary problem with respect to attribution of purpose to a failure to act.

Legislatures fail to act for many reasons. The decision not to proceed with proposed legislation may well be one on the merits, but it may well also reflect political wisdom—perhaps fear of offending powerful political interest groups, or belief that the question cannot be handled properly given the other demands on the legislators' time. Hence, reading significance into failure to act is risky business. As one court put it, "Legislative silence is a Delphic divination", Alabama–Tennessee Natural Gas Co. v. Federal Power Com'n (1966). Or, as Justice Frankfurter wrote in Helvering v. Hallock (1940), "To explain the cause of non-action by Congress when Congress itself sheds no light is to venture into speculative unrealities * * *. [W]e walk on quicksand when we try to find in the absence of corrective legislation a controlling legal principle."

Lack of probative value is not the only objection to reliance on legislative inaction. Such reliance also denies the proper place of the Executive in the law making process. Cleveland v. United States (1946) (Rutledge, J., dissenting). A bill, after all, cannot become law without the approval of the Executive (or the overriding of a veto). If effect is given legislative inaction then the Executive has been denied a chance to say that he disagrees. In effect, to read significance into inaction, as Hart and Sacks (supra § 4.2) suggest, is to act as if the legislature has passed a bill not to act. Of course, no such bill could become law without the Executive having a chance to veto it, but reliance on legislative failure to adopt proposed legislation in effect converts non-existent bills into law without executive input into the process.

a. *Legislation by Inaction*

Nevertheless, courts do pay a good deal of attention to what happens in the legislature. In Cooper v. Swoap (1974), for example, the court struck down an administrative regulation designed to "add" to a welfare bill a provision that had three times been voted down by the legislature. Clearly, the court in *Cooper* correctly identified the legislature's belief on the desirability of the challenged provision. No better evidence of legislative intent could have been found. But what of *executive* intent? Would the Governor have approved the bill if it had contained an express provision forbidding what the agency tried to do? If he would not have done so, which branch would have won the resulting political struggle? We do not know, but the decision in *Cooper* does not concern itself with such questions.

That does not mean the proposed legislation that failed of adoption is without value in the interpretive process. Especially useful to the court are those cases in which a bill's failure was contemporaneous with the adoption of related legislation, for the difference between the legislation as enacted and the legislation as introduced may shed some light on legislative goals. Especially informative would be a comparison of successive drafts of legislation; asking why each had been modified would help answer questions concerning legislative goals.

b. Action by Acquiescence

An even more dubious use of legislative silence occurs in cases in which the court bases its decision on the failure of the legislature to overturn a judicial interpretation of a statute. A famous example is Monell v. New York City Dept. of Social Services (1978), in which the Court partially relied on Congressional failure to overturn the effects of an earlier decision. In the implied remedy cases (see § 4.23), the courts have looked to the absence of Congressional intent on that issue in deciding whether it would be proper to imply a remedy. Yet attaching significance to an empty legislative record is a difficult argument to sustain. One effort to do so is Justice Black's opinion in The Boys Markets, Inc. v. Retail Clerk's Union (1970). There, the Supreme Court overruled an earlier decision, Sinclair Refining Co. v. Atkinson (1962). Dissenting in *Boys Markets,* Justice Black argued that *Sinclair Refining* contained an "invitation to legislative action", and that Congress' failure to act in the years since that decision "indicate[s] at least a willingness to leave the law as *Sinclair* has construed it. It seems to me highly inappropriate for this Court now * * * to enact the amendment that Congress has refused to adopt."

The problem with Justice Black's argument is that Congress has no constitutional obligation to accept the "invitation" extended to it in *Sinclair Refining*. It may refuse to do so for any number of reasons, good and bad: It may not be sure of the correct result, it may confidently expect the Court to correct its error, it may view attempted change as futile because the President will veto any change, it may be preoccupied with other matters, or it may simply fear the political consequences of any decision. All of those reasons are part of the political independence of Congress, an independence that is diminished when significance attaches to failure to accept an invitation to act.

There are other objections to reliance on legislative silence. Sometimes it seems to be a cloak for the court's lack of consideration of the issue at hand. In addition, it is a tool used inconsistently, brought only when convenient. One perceptive judge has said, "The doctrine of acquiescence by silence is at best a scapegoat doctrine * * *." Vincent v. Pabst Brewing Co. (1970) (Hallows, C.J., dissenting). Or, as Justice Douglas observed, "We do not think * * * that we can properly place on the shoulders of Congress the burden of the Court's own error." Girouard v. United States (1946). More judges should recognize the truth of those observations.

§ 5.22 Statutes and Administrative Interpretation

Congress commits a very large body of law to administrative agencies for implementation and enforcement. The agencies interpret a statute by issuing regulations and by adjudicating controversies. Courts often review those two forms of decision; in doing so they must determine the deference, if any, to be accorded the interpretive gloss the agency has placed on the statute. In doing so, the judges have drawn an important distinction between legislative and interpretive regulations.

Legislative Regulations. A long line of authority holds that so-called "legislative" regulations adopted by an agency will not be set aside unless they are "arbitrary, capricious, or irrational." Batterton v. Francis (1977). A key inquiry here is the scope of delegation from the legislature to the agency. In the *Batterton* case, for example, the Court found that Congress had "delegated" to the administrator "the power to prescribe standards for what constitutes unemployment for purposes of AFDC–UF eligibility." As a consequence, review of the administrator's interpretation was limited to the question of whether the agency had been delegated authority, whether the agency followed proper procedures in promulgating its regulation, and whether some basis for the regulation could be found.

A legislative or "substantive" (as it is sometimes called) regulation, the Court noted in *Batterton,* then, is one issued pursuant to a legislative directive giving the agency, "rather than * * * the courts, the primary responsibility for interpreting the statutory term. In exercising that responsibility, the Secretary adopts regulations with legislative effect." When that happens, the regulations have the force of law; a violator, for example, can be criminally prosecuted. In such a case, the court's role is limited to judicial review of the law established by the agency.

Interpretive Regulations. To the extent that agency decisions are not predicated upon delegated power to "make law" they are generally said to be "interpretive". An interpretation of a statute can occur either by regulation (the agency's view of the governing statute) or by adjudication. Again the question arises, how much deference should a court extend to the agency's view of the situation? As might be expected, the quick answer is, "It depends." Refining that answer requires consideration of several factors.

The legislature has given the agency power in order to achieve certain ends. Its initial decisions may reflect contemporary understanding of the whole legislative scheme. In addition, it has an overview of the whole area that a court, dealing with the isolated portions seen in litigation, does not. Most agency decisions never reach the courts; the job of insuring consistency in administrative decision-making, therefore, must fall primarily on the agency; judicial intrusion, because it is infrequent, must be discrete. Further, the agency often possesses technical expertise not available to the judiciary. For those reasons agency interpretation should be accorded a good deal of weight.

Unless the agency has been delegated law making power, however, a court bears final responsibility for the construction of the statute. The court must decide whether the action falls within the goals set by the legislature. And, of course, the court must bear more than final responsibility for the manner in which the statute is interpreted, for it must also supervise the agencies. An agency may become over-zealous. It may not itself be using proper interpretive techniques, necessitating instruction in that area by a court. Thus, deferral to agency action must be tempered by realism concerning agency behavior. Finally, the stringency of review has differed depending on whether the issue is one that courts feel confident to handle.

In Chevron, U.S.A., Inc. v. Natural Resources Defense Council (1984), the Supreme Court enunciated a highly deferential standard of review of an agency's interpretation of statutes. The Court set forth a two-step test for determining whether an administrative agency's interpretation of its authorizing statute is valid. First, the reviewing court must determine whether the statute specifically addresses the issue in question. If it does not, the court then determines whether the agency's interpretation of the statute as it relates to the issue is reasonable.

In *Chevron,* the Court had to determine whether the Environmental Protection Agency had complied with an air pollution control statute in developing regulations for new or modified major statutory sources of air pollution. The EPA had permitted polluters to use a "bubble" approach that established an entire plant rather than each smokestack in the plant as the air pollution source and permitted adjustment of emissions within the plant.

The Court observed that if Congress had addressed the precise question at issue, that intent would govern. A court would employ "traditional tools of statutory interpretation" to determine whether Congress' intent was clear. The Court first looked to the language of the statute and then to its legislative history and found that Congress did not specifically address the issue of whether a "bubble" policy was appropriate.

The Court held that if Congress had not directly addressed an issue in a statute, "the court does not simply impose its own construction on the statute, as would be necessary in the absence of an administrative interpretation." It is with respect to this latter point that some commentators believe the Court dramatically departed from its prior standard of review. That is, *Chevron* can be viewed as a step backward by the judicial branch from closely scrutinizing an administrative agency's interpretation of its authorizing statute. Compare, for example, Justice Jackson's opinion in Skidmore v. Swift & Co. (1944);

> We consider that the rulings, interpretations and opinions of the Administrator under this Act, while not controlling upon the courts by reason

of their authority, do constitute a body of experience and informed judgment to which courts and litigants may properly resort for guidance. The weight of such a judgment in a particular case will depend upon the thoroughness evident in its consideration, the validity of its reasoning, its consistency with earlier and later pronouncements, and all those factors which give it power to persuade, if lacking power to control.

A number of commentators also view *Chevron* as recognizing that interpretation of ambiguous statutes involves policy decisions, a task more properly accomplished by the branches of government responsive to the electorate. Nevertheless, *Chevron* can also be viewed as a recognition that Congress may have wanted to avoid choosing a solution to a specific problem, relying instead on the agency's expertise (and perhaps its lack of political accountability) to provide an answer. In that sense, *Chevron* can be seen as fulfilling congressional policy.

§ 5.23   The Effect of Private Interpretation

Most statutes are not directed primarily at official bodies such as courts and administrative agencies, but are instead designed to influence and control the conduct of private parties. In construing a statute with such an aim it is imperative that there be inquiry into the construction placed upon the law by the public who must work with it.

One reason for paying attention to private interpretation is that some statutes are expressly designed to give effect to private decisions. Thus they invite courts to rely on the construction of the statute by those to whom they are addressed. Article 2 of the Uniform Commercial Code (dealing with the sale of goods) is an example. Karl Llewellyn, the principal draftsman of Article 2, wrote many of the provisions so that they would insure that courts would interpret arrangements involving the sale of goods in a "commercially reasonable" manner—a very common phrase in the Code. Richard Danzig, in A Comment on the Jurisprudence of the Uniform Commercial Code, 27 Stan.L. Rev. 621 (1975), explained that the goal of such phrasing was to insure that courts would focus on commercial practice in resolving disputes. Because commercial or mercantile interpretation was explicitly invited by the Code, a court must be careful to evaluate the reliance placed by private parties on their "commercially reasonable" arrangements.

Reliance can also take the form of a common way of *doing* something, even though that way may differ from the statute's apparent mandate. In Mitchell v. Van Pelt (1954), for example, a statute directed an administrator to file proof of notification of creditors "within thirty (30) days of the completion of said publication"; a creditor contended that until that notice was filed the statute of limitations against the creditor did not begin to run. The court took notice of authority supporting the creditor's position, but then added:

> The construction sought by appellant * * * necessarily calls for a change in accepted practice which will result in substantial expense to the public. Contrary construction of the statute will not unsettle the affairs of persons who have relied upon the law as it has been accepted and applied by a majority of the lawyers and courts in this state.

The court then held the 30–day provision to be merely directory and that the limitations period began to run against the creditor from the time notice was published.

The *Mitchell* court advanced other reasons for its holding, especially the absence of any affirmative reasons that would be served by giving effect to the creditor's position. Common understanding of a statute, at least if it would not thwart a legislative purpose, can be a significant consideration in statutory interpretation.

An important form of private interpretation is the construction placed on a statute by the bar, for it is there that expectations are most likely to be built upon the construction. In McBrien v. Warden (1966), for example, the court emphasized the legal community's understanding of the statute since 1846, when it was adopted. "A construction by bench and bar alike over such a long period is entitled to great weight."

An occasional statute reflects legislative exasperation with judicial failure to recognize the force of private interpretation. An example is an amendment to the Fair Labor Standards Act, 29 U.S.C.A. § 251(a), which begins: "The Congress hereby finds the [Act] has been interpreted judicially in disregard of long-established customs, practices, and contracts * * *." Obviously, Congress believed the Act should be interpreted in accordance with "long-established customs." Doing so is especially important in the case of a statute like the Fair Labor Standards Act which regulates a myriad of labor practices in countless work places. It would be impossible for the Act to provide sufficient detail to cover all possible situations. Instead, the effective working of the statute must depend upon workers and employers reaching practical solutions within the statutory framework.

§ 5.24 Stare Decisis Revisited

Earlier judicial constructions of a statute also create popular understanding of what that statute means. The question of precedent and the weight to be attached to it in deciding later cases was discussed in Chapter Four. To review briefly, a precedent creates a presumption in favor of the earlier decision; to test the strength of that presumption a court must consider the desirability of the proposed changes and the factors that push against overruling—chiefly the reliance that may have been placed on the precedent. The question addressed in this section is whether that analysis of the problem should change when the precedent under consideration is judicial construction of a statute. Generally, courts and commentators have agreed that the problems involved in evaluating precedent in statutory cases do not differ materially from the problems found in common law decisions. Although there are numerous cases in which a court has reversed itself on a question of construction, little attention has been paid to the question of *stare decisis* in this area. There are, however, occasional flashes of illumination. An example is Justice Stevens' concurring opinion in Runyon v. McCrary (1976). The majority in *Runyon* held that § 1 of the Civil Rights Act of 1866 (codified now in 42 U.S.C.A. §§ 1981–1982) prohibits racial discrimination in private schools. That decision was predicated upon the Court's earlier decision in Jones v. Alfred H. Mayer Co. (1968), which had held that another part of the 1866 Act prohibited private racial discrimination in the sale of property. Justice Stevens, along with the majority, believed that *Jones* controlled *Runyon*. Unlike the majority, however, Stevens believed *Jones* to have been decided incorrectly and that if he were writing on a clean slate he would have held for the defendant in *Jones*. He then proceeded to examine the question of whether *Jones* should be overruled: "There are two reasons which favor overruling. First, as I have already stated, my conviction that *Jones* was wrongly decided is firm. Second, it is extremely unlikely that reliance upon *Jones* has been so extensive that this Court is foreclosed from overruling it. Cf. Flood v. Kuhn, 407 U.S. 258 [1972] * * *." Justice Stevens' inquiry into the

correctness of the precedent and the reliance interests implicated in overruling the precedent is similar to the inquiry made when a court reexamines
a common law decision.

Justice Stevens then turned to counter-arguments that favored the continuation of the rule in
Jones v. Mayer. He began by noting the general
desirability of saving judicial resources by not re-
opening settled issues. Next, he examined the
likely impact of a decision to overrule *Jones*:

> [E]ven if *Jones* did not accurately reflect the
> sentiments of the Reconstruction Congress, it
> surely accords with the prevailing sense of jus-
> tice today.

> The policy of the Nation as formulated by the
> Congress in recent years has moved constantly
> in the direction of eliminating racial segregation
> in all sectors of society. This Court has given a
> sympathetic and liberal construction to such leg-
> islation. For the Court now to overrule *Jones*
> would be a significant step backwards, with ef-
> fects that would not have arisen from a correct
> decision in the first instance.

Although this argument looks like one based on
the desirability of stability in law, in fact it is more
interesting than that, for it centers not on reliance
on the earlier decision by an individual, but on
reliance by *society* as a whole on the decision in
Jones. Because Stevens believed that the orderly
development of society would be upset by overruling *Jones* he declined to do so.

Not all cases that raise the question of continued existence of precedent in statutory interpretation are decided by opinions as sophisticated as Justice Stevens'. Flood v. Kuhn (1972), referred to by Stevens in *Runyon,* involved the continuing saga of the relationship between baseball and the antitrust laws. In Federal Base Ball Club of Baltimore v. National League of Professional Base Ball Clubs (1922), the Court held that the Sherman Act did not apply because baseball was not "interstate commerce." The question next came before the Court in Toolson v. New York Yankees, Inc. (1953). During the interval between the two cases, the Supreme Court had substantially redefined Congressional power to legislate under the commerce clause so that there could be no question that baseball was indeed interstate commerce. *Toolson,* however, retained baseball's favored antitrust status. Two decades later, Curt Flood, an outfielder for the St. Louis Cardinals, objected (understandably) to being traded to the Philadelphia Phillies (which in turn sold its rights to Flood to the then Washington Senators). Flood's suit challenged the legality of baseball's reserve clause. The challenge failed, despite the fact that other professional sports (e.g., hockey, football, boxing, etc.) had been subjected to the antitrust laws, and despite recognition by the Court that continued exemption for baseball from those laws was without foundation and "aberrational." Unfortunately, nowhere in the majority opinion in *Flood* (or in its predecessor *Toolson*) was there even a pretense at inquiry into the *quality* of baseball's reliance on the earlier decisions or the possibility of overruling the judicial exemption prospectively. Instead, the decision merely *differentiated* baseball from similar industries without *distinguishing* it from them.* The need to distinguish baseball is, of course, the necessary inquiry. It is wrong to continue a precedent that is "aberrational" and which concededly does not treat like persons in like fashion. Given the other antitrust/professional sports decisions it would seem the Court's duty was plain—baseball should have been given the same status as other sports. The question, then, was simply one of whether *Toolson* should have been overruled prospectively. That question can and should have been decided in reasoned fashion, just as a court does when overruling a purely common law decision. A decision in favor of Curt Flood would have been a signal that all problems have to be evaluated constantly in light of how a statute works in the context of current problems. Doing so would help fulfill the ultimate goal of statutory interpretation, to achieve the goals sought by the Legislature when the law was adopted.

Not all commentators believe, however, that a court should be free to change its mind on ques-

* My students explain the opinion in *Flood* by pointing out that the Sherman Act had run up against a fundamental value of American society—baseball, the national pastime—and should not be read as changing that principle (see § 5.16). The opinion certainly provides evidence to support that reading: during the course of it Justice Blackmun listed several dozen great players, recounted the history of the game, and recited the poem "Tinkers to Evers to Chance."

tions of interpretation. Justice Black, dissenting in The Boys Markets, Inc. v. Retail Clerk's Union, (1970) (see supra, § 5.21), urged that a decision construing a statute should not be overruled absent "exceptional" circumstances; to do so the Court would have to interject itself too much into the lawmaking process. Edward Levi, former Dean and Attorney General, has urged that, unless the matter is "vital", a rule of strict *stare decisis* is appropriate in cases applying statutes. Levi, An Introduction to Legal Reasoning, 15 U.Chi.L.Rev. 501 (1948). He grounded this argument on the basic arbitrariness of a search for something that normally does not exist—legislative "intention." Hence, in order to limit decision-making that would necessarily be arbitrary, Dean Levi believed adherence to precedent to be the proper approach.

There are several problems with that argument. First, and most important, its major premise seems wide of the mark. A statute *does* seek to achieve certain ends, for it is a purposeful act. Any decision that does not try to implement those ends denies proper scope to the wishes of a coordinate branch of government (see § 5.3). Because a court can mistake those wishes it must be free to correct itself in the light of hindsight and better information. If it does not do so it will continue to frustrate the achievement of legislative goals.

In addition to the constitutional problem, it is necessary at times to change a precedent in order to achieve fairness and uniformity. Again, baseball provides an example. In *Toolson* the Court continued baseball's favored antitrust status "without re-examination of the underlying issues." If the Court had re-examined the issues, the result, given changes in the character of baseball, the scope of the Sherman Act, and its application in similar situations, would surely have been different. In *Flood* the push to uniformity should have been irresistible; it is outrageous to pass off baseball's favored status when compared with other sports as a mere "aberration." Failure—twice—to inquire into the validity of precedent led to bad decision-making.

There are, however, times when the push for uniformity and consistency of application will make it difficult for a court to change its view of a statute. Indeed, many statutes with long histories acquire a life of their own and little attention is paid to questions of "statutory interpretation." They have in fact become part of the "common law." Examples here are legion; most prominent, perhaps, are the Parliamentary enactments "received" as law by the newly independent colonies (see § 2.3), such as the Statute of Frauds (1677) or the Statute of Wills (1540). Other examples are the Sherman Antitrust Act (1890), 15 U.S.C.A. § 1 *et seq.*, and, more recently, the basic definition of "income" in the Internal Revenue Code, 26 U.S. C.A. § 61 (1954). It would be very difficult for a court interpreting any of those statutes to reopen basic lines of construction. To a large extent, therefore, interpretation becomes frozen through a long history of application.

§ 5.25 Statutes and Changing Problems

A statute often addresses problems whose dimensions change over time. A court must decide whether the old bottles corked by the legislature can pour new wine. Although the problem looks tricky, it is not necessarily so, and courts have not been reluctant to distribute new vintages.

Commonly, this problem arises under the influence of technological change. Legislators write statutes to reflect their contemporary circumstances. Should the coverage of the statute respond to those changes? Does a statute dealing with the "press", for example, enacted in 1820 apply to the electronic media? Does an ordinance requiring a license for a tavern to show movies require a license for a television? Courts deciding such issues must determine what purpose the law sought to achieve and whether it would be furthered by application to the new technology involved in the case before the court.

The transition from the horse and buggy to the automobile provided a number of illustrations. Typical were the cases involving a statutory exemption from a creditor's levy. In McMullen v. Shields (1934), the statute exempted "one cart or wagon." The court held that the exemption extended to an automobile that had been attached by a creditor. The majority believed the statutory

exemption of a wagon was designed to permit a
family to do necessary hauling, and thus exemption of the car was necessary in order to satisfy
statutory goals: "The Legislature was not so much
concerned with the name of the thing exempted as
it was with the use to which it was put." Most
courts agreed with that result, although a contrary
conclusion was reached in some cases. An example is Prater v. Reichman (1916). There, the court
found the luxurious nature of an automobile made
it a "different class of vehicle" from those expressly exempted. "It was invented to meet the needs
of a different class of citizenship * * * [which] is
usually well able to pay [its] debts." Thus, finding
the statutory purpose is of vital importance in
determining the impact of changed circumstances
on a statute's coverage, thereby permitting legislative goals to be fulfilled even in an evolving society.

§ 5.26 Desuetude

Desuetude, the abrogation of an obsolete statute
through judicial action, is grounded in the theory
that prolonged nonenforcement of a law effectively
repeals it. Desuetude had (and continues to have)
its widest influence in the law of Scotland. As
developed there, a statute could not be judicially
repealed through mere non-use or non-enforcement. The statute in question must not have been
enforced at all for a substantial period of time,
during which the opportunity for enforcement

arose. Further, a new practice contrary to the
statute must have arisen and been in wide regular
use for an appreciable length of time. It is unclear
what the nature of the contrary acts or practice
must be; whether they can consist of continued
non-punishment or moral approval of the community.

Desuetude has not been widely accepted either in
England or in the United States. In this country it
was used to some extent by state courts in the
nineteenth century with regard to English statutes
that had been applied in the colonies, and to older
state statutes.

The Supreme Court flatly rejected desuetude in
District of Columbia v. John R. Thompson Co., Inc.
(1953). Acts of the Legislative Assembly of the
District of Columbia of 1872 and 1873 had made it
a crime to refuse service to anyone on account of
race or color.   Apparently, the defendant in
Thompson was the first person prosecuted under
the statutes during the 75 years they had been on
the books. Reversing the decision below, the Court
held that failure of the executive branch to enforce
a law does not result in its *de facto* modification or
repeal. Writing for the majority, Justice Douglas
noted that "the repeal of laws is as much a legislative function as their enactment."

Desuetude, however, may have some indirect
bearing on decisions. Use of a statute after a long
period of quiescence may suggest due process or

equal protection problems and continued non-usage may also be significant.

An example is Poe v. Ullman (1961). The plaintiffs in *Poe* had sought a declaratory judgment that an 1879 Connecticut statute which prohibited the use of birth control was unconstitutional. They alleged that though they had not been prosecuted under the statute, the local prosecutor had stated that he would prosecute any violations of state law. The Court held that no justiciable issue had been presented because there was no real threat of prosecution under the statute. The Court noted tha 'there had not been a prosecution under the statute for 80 years, that contraceptives were sold openly in drugstores in the state, and that there was an "undeviating policy of nullification by Connecticut of its anti-contraception laws." In short, the fact of non-enforcement deprived the controversy of the necessary immediacy because there was no real threat of prosecution. (The *Poe* Court made no attempt to reconcile this decision with *Thompson,* its own recent precedent.) *Poe* suggests that some uses may still be found for desuetude.

One solution to the problem of the archaic statute is to provide that after a certain period (say, ten years) the statute expires unless it is re-enacted. A number of states have passed such "sunset" laws; they are particularly popular in administrative law. Guido Calabresi, in A Common Law for the Age of Statutes (1982), has suggested another solution. Courts, he argued, should have the power to invalidate obsolete statutes. This proposal has intrigued many scholars, but its obvious constitutional (separation of powers) and practical (how does a court know when a statute is obsolete?) difficulties have so far prevented it from receiving judicial favor.

§ 5.27   The Equity of the Statute Revisited

An earlier section (§ 4.23) discussed at some length the notion that a statute can serve as a source of policy for a court even though the statute by its own terms does not apply. The most common example is the implication of a civil remedy from a criminal or administrative statute, although other examples, such as the Married Women's Acts, can be found. Early writers on statutory interpretation referred to a statute's "equity" that a court would invoke in making that decision.

That concept recognizes that lawmaking is a joint enterprise in which legislature and court can complement one another. Each builds on what the other has done, both with the same goal of achieving a better society, a task that changes constantly as society evolves. Each possesses advantages for performing that task, and each can learn from the other. Legislation represents policy identified as desirable by the representative branch of government. As such it is entitled to the full respect of the courts. The classic statement on this use of a statute's equity comes from Plowden, a reporter of English decisions in the late sixteenth century: "It is a good way, when you peruse a statute, to suppose that the lawmaker is present, and that you have asked him the question you want to know touching the equity, then you must give yourself such an answer as you imagine he would have done; if he had been present." That advice sounds good today.

§ 5.28 A Concluding Note

The court's first job in questions of interpretation is to determine the purpose of the legislature (and executive) in passing the statute. In moving beyond the language itself in the searching for purpose, the court should evaluate proffered evidence in terms of its probative value. The next task is to determine if those purposes would be furthered by application in the case at bar. Finally, the court must consider whether developments after the statute was enacted should affect its interpretation. Here, the interpretation by other courts, by agencies, and by private persons must be considered. Above all else, the court must remember that its job is to achieve as best it can the goals set by the legislature in adopting the statute.

CHAPTER SIX
CONSTITUTIONAL INTERPRETATION
PART A
BACKGROUND

§ 6.1 Introduction

After many years of relative quiet, the field of constitutional interpretation has been subject to much ferment in the past dozen years. Many reasons have driven that renewal of interest, but perhaps the most important was the dramatic revolution in constitutional law wrought by the Supreme Court during the period in which Earl Warren was Chief Justice (1953–69). As the substantive content of that revolution drew increasing criticism, attention also focused on the Court's method of interpreting the Constitution. Those who approved of the Warren Court's decisions, of course, countered with arguments as to why the decisions *were* compatible with the Constitution. The resulting debate on proper interpretive technique has been vigorous, indeed.

This Chapter examines problems of constitutional interpretation. The central question involves fidelity to the original document: Should the meaning of the Constitution be limited to the document as drafted, or should the document be permitted to "grow" with changing times? Both sides of that debate will be examined. The Chapter then concludes with an analysis of *stare decisis* in constitutional law. The focus will be on methods of interpreting the Federal Constitution; the discussion applies equally well, however, to state constitutions.

§ 6.2 Comparing Statutes and Constitutions

One major difference between statute and constitution arises from the comparative difficulty of amending the latter. Typically, "constitutional" majorities greater than 50% are required, and sometimes other obstacles are placed in the way of an amendment to slow the pace of its adoption. Imposing such difficult requirements for adoption helps insure that the basic law of the nation or state will not be lightly altered without widespread support.

The other major difference between statute and constitution is more important. The constitution *is* the basic law of the state or nation and all three branches of government must operate within the limits that it sets. Thus, the courts in constitutional interpretation cases need not, and do not, defer as an institutional matter to the legislature, as is the case with statutory interpretation. This does not mean that the legislature cannot be looked to for guidance on difficult questions, or that legislation is not entitled to a presumption of validity, but the final decision is for the judicial branch. More important, courts, both state and federal, began at the start of the nineteenth century to assert a power to declare legislation *un*constitutional and, therefore, invalid. Advanced somewhat tentatively at first as part of the Court's need to apply *all* of the law—including the Constitution itself—to a case properly before the Court, the power to review legislation for constitutional defects eventually led the Supreme Court to declare itself the "ultimate interpreter of the Constitution." Baker v. Carr (1962).

How have these differences affected questions of constitutional interpretation? Constitutional decision-making is a very sensitive task: Constitutional decisions are difficult to overturn; they may also invalidate choices made by the democratically responsive branches of government. Judges, therefore, must be careful to devise an acceptable and coherent method of solving constitutional problems that they are willing to apply consistently. The need for that kind of approach, of course, is strong in statutory interpretation; the need is even greater when it is the Constitution that is being examined.

§ 6.3 The Debate

The primary dispute in this area has been the question of how much fidelity is owed to the "Original Understanding" (a commonly used phrase) of the framers of the original document and succeeding amendments. Some would use an approach rooted in language and history, believing it improper to exercise the awesome power of judicial review in any other way. Without the limits imposed on judges by words or history, it is argued, the courts will have vast power to restructure society, a power checked only by the doubtful threats of amendment and impeachment. Such "strict constructionists" (another popular phrase) also argue that a consensus exists that their method of interpretation is the proper one. Hugo Black and Antonin Scalia have been the Justices most commonly associated with this point of view in recent years.

Opposed to the "strict constructionists" are those who believe in a Constitution continually adapted by the judiciary to serve new challenges posed by an ever-evolving society. The "present" Constitution to those persons is, to some significant extent, "unwritten," in the sense that the meaning of the document can be found primarily in the case law. Because the case law responds to constant pressure from litigants for the Court to solve constantly-changing problems, the meaning of the Constitution adapts to the pressures placed upon it. The text of the Constitution serves as a repository of enduring values, but one whose lessons and applications can change over time.

On this debate see generally Farber, The Originalism Debate: A Guide for the Perplexed, 49 Ohio St.L.J. 1085 (1989); Kay, Adherence to the Original Intentions in Constitutional Adjudication: Three

Objections and a Response, 82 Nw.U.L.Rev. 226 (1988).

PART B
THE CASE FOR ORIGINALISM

§ 6.4   The Debate Renewed

"The whole aim of construction, as applied to a provision of the Constitution, is to discover the meaning, to ascertain and give effect to the intent of its framers and the people who adopted it." That statement by Justice Sutherland, dissenting in Home Bldg. & Loan Ass'n v. Blaisdell (1934), is one of the most widely quoted arguments for originalism. That statement reflects a belief that the original meaning of the Constitution is the only meaning that matters. Proponents of originalism proffer a number of reasons to justify their position.

a.   The Written Constitution

Perhaps the most famous justification for originalism was given by Chief Justice Marshall in Marbury v. Madison (1803), the case which established the power of the Supreme Court to declare invalid acts of Congress that are "repugnant" to the Constitution. Marshall emphasized in *Marbury* that we have a "written Constitution," a fact that he believed strongly supported the exercise of judicial review. This argument assumes that the

Constitution was *written* in order to give it a more or less precise or fixed meaning; anyone could read the document, in other words, and determine whether any governmental action—by Congress, Court, or President—was constitutionally permissible. The meaning of an unwritten constitution (or of one whose words bore no fixed meaning), in contrast, could not easily be determined; case reports and a good deal of historical material would have to be read and much scholarly analysis would be needed for *that* job. The complexity and ambiguity of that task necessarily undermines the very reasons why we do have a *written* Constitution.

b. *Majority Rule*

Another main prop of originalist thinking focuses on the "anti-democratic" nature of judicial review. When the Supreme Court declares a federal law unconstitutional, it frustrates the will of the democratically chosen branches of government— the Congress and the President. That gives rise to the following question: What gives judges, an elite, non-elected group drawn from the upper class of the legal profession, the right to thwart the will of the people's representatives? Proponents of originalism maintain that only a clear-cut violation of what the Constitution *means* can justify a declaration of unconstitutionality. That, in turn, requires that there be certainty concerning the meaning and proper application of the text—a certainty that only originalism can supply. Because the

Court, unlike the other two branches, is not democratically responsible, it should be quite reluctant to invoke its power unless it has no other choice given the language of the document. Originalism, therefore, serves to restrain the Court's freedom in a way that more open-ended interpretive techniques do not.

c. A Sacred Text?

Such concerns have led to a strong focus on the actual *text* of the Constitution. Few originalists, however, are willing to ignore other relevant evidence. Even an ardent foe of the use of historical materials in statutory interpretation such as Justice Scalia is willing to use extrinsic evidence on at least some occasions. See, e.g., Morrison v. Olson (1988) (dissenting) (use of *The Federalist Papers* in a separation of powers case).

Some originalists would apply a version of the Plain Meaning Rule (see § 5.6) to questions of constitutional interpretation. The problems involved with using the Plain Meaning Rule in statutory interpretation do not disappear, however, when the Constitution is the text in question. All plain meaning arguments require one to believe that meaning can be separated from context, and that phrases like "due process" or Congressional power "to regulate Commerce" can be interpreted without knowing their history and purpose. A refusal to look at context is as wrong in constitutional interpretation as it is in statutory interpretation.

d. Continuing Ratification

Finally, originalist interpretation keeps faith with what is probably the popular understanding, it is argued, of how the Constitution should be interpreted. Expressed somewhat differently, the average person would believe that the Constitution should be interpreted according to its original meaning. Originalism, therefore, is compatible with a kind of continuing ratification by the people both of the Constitution and the method by which it should be interpreted.

§ 6.5 Problems With Originalism

Although an excellent case can be made for originalism, the concept suffers from serious drawbacks. These can be placed into two general categories. The first deals with difficulties in ascertaining what it was the framers really did. The second involves a different set of concerns: the meaning derived from the text does not correspond to the needs of modern life; the reader, to put it crudely, would prefer a meaning different from the original one.

§ 6.6 Textual Difficulties

The preceding Chapter in this *Nutshell* discussed the problem of deriving meaning from statutory text. The lessons learned there generally apply also in the constitutional area. There are also some important differences.

a. Whose Meaning?

A problem peculiar to this area involves determining whose meaning should control. Consider the original Constitution. It was drafted by several dozen "framers" in Philadelphia in 1787. Congress forwarded it to the states for ratification. Eleven states ratified it fairly quickly, and a new government was formed. When we search for original meaning are we interested in the meaning of those who drafted it or of those who ratified it? Or both?

The overwhelming concern of both judges and commentators has been to find the meaning that the document would be given by those who drafted it—the framers for the original Constitution and Congress for later amendments. The issue is a good deal more complicated than that, however, for should we not be more concerned with the meaning of those who have the power to *ratify* it? After all, *their* approval is necessary for the proposal to become law. That does not mean that the framers' views are irrelevant; their deliberations can be considered analogous to those of a legislative committee: informative and helpful, but not definitive.

Determining the group whose meaning interests us is not just an idle question, for the understanding of what a provision was thought to accomplish (that is, its meaning) can change as it is talked about during the ratification process. A prime example is *The Federalist Papers,* a series of newspaper articles originally written to persuade voters in New York to approve the Constitution. They contain a comprehensive and well-developed theory of government, parts of which might have surprised others who sat in the Convention. Written by Alexander Hamilton, James Madison, and John Jay, *The Federalist Papers,* at least as a whole, had little impact on the ratification process outside New York (one of the last states to ratify the Constitution). Nevertheless, the Supreme Court has relied very heavily on *The Federalist Papers* for help in construing the Constitution.

b.   *How Accurate Is the Record?*

Assume you are interested in determining the intent of the drafters or of the ratifiers; how do you find evidence of that intent and how reliable is the evidence? The records of the Philadelphia Convention of 1787, for example, are spotty. Our best source of information is James Madison's notes of the Convention where he served as Secretary; although their accuracy has been questioned, they seem accepted today as generally reliable. But they are not comprehensive, and the records left by other participants do not fill in very many blanks. See generally Hutson, The Creation of the Constitution: The Integrity of the Documentary Record, 65 Tex.L.Rev. 1 (1986).

There is also a problem with negative history. What of those who *opposed* ratification? The record of opposition of prominent opponents such as Luther Martin, Elbridge Gerry, and Patrick Henry is even less complete. And if their views could be known, would we care? After all, a dissenter's purpose, as discussed earlier (§ 5.11), is not to show how something will work, but rather why it *will not* work. Of course, that argument has another side; the tendency of those who favor ratification would be to disguise or paper over possible future difficulties—and dissenters like the three Anti–Federalists mentioned above can expose those problems, both for their audience as well as for the future.

c. Finding the Evidence

Another problem involves accessibility and volume. Determining just what the legislature and executive have said is difficult enough; attempting to fix meaning in important cases based on the sometimes fragmentary evidence surviving over two hundred years makes the task extremely arduous on occasion. Beyond the problem of fragmentation is the problem of determining what the language used by the framers actually meant two centuries ago. This is a problem long recognized by historians: Can we really determine how those who lived long ago thought and used language? The words are deceptively familiar, but the subtleties they convey may have changed.

Then there is the problem of volume. If we are concerned with the views of the ratifiers as well as of the drafters, for example, the records of the ratification proceedings of all of the states must be examined in order to ascertain meaning. That obviously can take a lot of time and money—assuming that any records are even available. Is this a game that can only be played by the wealthy (including the government)? Moreover, the volume of evidence may make it *more* difficult to sort out meaning. Ambiguity may be easier to find (or at least to create) when there is more, rather than less, evidence. These difficulties obviously explain why evidence of interest in case law and commentary seems to be derived almost exclusively from the drafters not from the ratifiers.

d. *What Did the Framers Think About Interpretation?*

Did the framers have a view concerning how their documents should be interpreted? This very important and usually overlooked question has finally received a good deal of scholarly attention. Consider, for example, what your view towards originalism might be if it were clear that the framers expected and wanted the document to grow and change with the times; if that were so, why would it make any sense to give controlling effect to the specific concerns of those who wrote and ratified the Constitution? In other words, if the framers did not want to limit the meaning of the Constitution to what it meant in 1787, how can an originalist be interested in original meaning?

The problem with asking this question is that constitution writing and constitutional interpretation were new exercises in 1787. Because there was little experience with constitutional government, there was, naturally enough, no theory as to *how* a constitution should be construed, and it was not a problem with which the Convention concerned itself.

This problem also has an ironic twist to it. Later constitutional amendments, such as the Fourteenth Amendment, were adopted at a time when lawyers and judges realized from their own experience that our governing document might be construed in an open-ended manner. Does that mean that the later amendments, at least, must be considered to have been enacted with an expectation that they will be interpreted loosely?

e. Continuing Ratification

Similarly, it is at least arguable that the people have come to expect that the judiciary *will* adapt the Constitution to changing times; if so, then there has been a kind of continuing ratification of a more open-ended method of interpretation. Moreover, it can also be argued that the people have ratified in that manner *specific* departures from original meaning.

§ 6.7 Problems With Originalism: The Need for a Modern Constitution

The problems described in the preceding section have led many to conclude that the originalists search for a meaning which cannot be found. More generally, however, critique of the originalist interpretation has focused on dissatisfaction with the results of originalism.

The Constitution was adopted by a generally elitist, pre-industrial, rural society in which only white men could vote. It would be astonishing if all of the solutions chosen by that society were compatible with today's needs and values. The Constitution does provide for change through the amendment process, of course, but the sheer difficulty of amending the document provides a strong argument based on expediency for empowering the judiciary to re-shape the Constitution. The framers neither foresaw nor planned the society we live in today. To some extent, therefore, the Constitution has become irrelevant or even harmful.

The Constitution says nothing at all about such contemporary issues as abortion, affirmative action, state aid to religious schools, reapportionment, and a number of other pressing problems of today. Yet, there is enormous pressure to have the Constitution say something about those issues. Americans have grown accustomed to framing issues in terms of a claim of personal right and then seeking to have a court enforce the claim—we expect the Constitution to protect our claims of right even if it has nothing explicit to say about them.

This notion of a "living Constitution" has a powerful appeal. Judges, independent and sophisticated thinkers, should have room to re-shape our organic law and make it better and fairer. Beguiling and compelling as that argument may be, however, it suffers from serious deficiencies.

a. The Amendment Process

The Constitution does provide specifically for change, but it makes any change difficult to achieve. Article V requires, therefore, that a proposed amendment be endorsed by two-thirds of Congress (or of a Constitutional Convention) and then be ratified by three-fourths of the States. These obstacles were imposed deliberately; it was thought that our basic law should not be amended unless there was very strong support across the nation for doing so. It was not a document to be changed lightly or for transient reasons. And it was the *people*—and not the judiciary—who were entrusted with the responsibility and power of making any necessary changes. All of this suggests that the judiciary should not circumvent the prescribed amendment process by changing the Constitution. Of course, that observation does not help us determine what it means to "change" the Constitution.

b. *Whose Values?*

A fundamental problem with the notion of a living Constitution involves determining the direction in which it should develop. What values should the judiciary use in rewriting the Constitution? Is there some body of natural law which can be drawn upon to make the Constitution better? What of religious beliefs; are they useful in this quest? If guidance can be found in religion or philosophy, what does a court do when those sources have different views? Or perhaps there is some "genius" of the American people which can be discovered and used to guide decision-making? Does the Constitution, in other words, represent a few fundamental values which courts can draw upon in order to reconcile what was done two hundred years ago with the needs of today?

The problem is not that these sources cannot provide guidance. The difficulty is that they give too many answers. Constitutional issues become difficult sometimes *because* different answers are quite possible. A wealth of possibilities raises again the problem of accountability: How can a judge choose among those possibilities and avoid the claim of ad hoc (or "result-oriented") decision-making? The challenge, to those who would depart from originalism, in other words, is whether they can find a principled method of selecting among those choices and thereby make the living Constitution compatible with the concept of reasoned elaboration.

c. Judicial Restraint

A last argument against judicial freedom to redo the Constitution involves the problem of judicial activism. Many believe that judges should not be reformers, and that the decision of the more democratic legislative and executive branches should not be set aside unless the Constitution "compels" that result. It is the *elected* bodies of government, and not the courts, who have been entrusted with the task of reforming our government. This is merely another way of saying that constitutional cases require courts to reflect upon their proper role in the scheme of government, to think about questions such as accountability and responsibility. For those who reject originalism the question might be put this way: If text and history do not restrain the judges, what will?

PART C
A MIDDLE WAY?

§ 6.8   Synthesis

Neither strict construction nor living Constitution represent prevailing attitudes towards the interpretation of the Constitution in litigation today. A middle way seems, instead, to prevail in practice, if not in theory. The Court cloaks most of its decisions in references to constitutional language and history. It tries to maintain ties with the past while also recognizing that the force of developments in both society and decisional law limit—or are believed to limit—the force to be given "original understanding." The text for this lesson comes from Chief Justice Marshall in McCulloch v. Maryland (1819) (with his emphasis): "We must never forget that it is a *constitution* we are expounding." In *McCulloch* Marshall compared our Constitution with the "prolixity" found in "legal codes," and observed that the Constitution was destined to endure for "ages to come." The Constitution, in other words, in order to endure, does not contain prolix provisions designed to cover every possible problem. Rather, its broad language sets forth principles which can be applied to particular problems. Perhaps the best way to introduce this concept is to refer to the "two-clause" theory.

As expounded by Justice Frankfurter, its most enthusiastic proponent, some clauses are explicit and "technical," others are composed of majestic generalities designed to permit accommodation between Constitution and changing economic and social conditions. In National Mut. Ins. Co. v. Tidewater Transfer Co. (1949), for example, Frankfurter contrasted the "precision" of constitutional provisions dealing with federal judicial power, with "[g]reat concepts" like the commerce and due process clauses. The "strict definitions" of the former clauses cannot change, but the meaning ascribed to the "vague and elastic" phrases was "purposely left to gather meaning from experience." In this way, the authority of Congress to legislate under the commerce clause, for example, could be expanded in the late 1930's to give virtually unlimited legislative power to Congress.

Although the "two-clause" theory is not accepted Supreme Court dogma, it explains much in recent constitutional decision-making. Some provisions *are* very elastic. "Due process" and "equal protection," for example, have proven supple instruments in the hands of Justices determined to reconcile organic law with perceived societal needs:

> It is of the very nature of a free society to advance in its standards of what is deemed reasonable and right. Representing as it does a living principle, due process is not confined within a permanent catalogue of what may at a given time be deemed the limits or the essentials of fundamental rights.

Wolf v. Colorado (1949). Of course, when it comes to resolving a specific case, it is questionable how much guidance can be found by examining "the very nature of a free society."

The key, then, is to find a method of harmonizing originalism and the many generalities of the original document with changing problems, so that the Constitution can last for "ages to come," even though it lacks the prolixity of a "legal code." The concept of "purpose," which was discussed in § 5.5 with respect to statutory interpretation, may provide an answer.

Katz v. United States (1967), provides an example. At issue there was the admissibility of evidence obtained by an electronic wiretap, made without a warrant. The majority found that one of the goals of the Fourth Amendment was to protect our expectations of privacy. That purpose obviously would be frustrated if the wiretapping at issue was legal, even though the framers, who of course knew nothing of wiretapping, could not have had any specific intent about its legality.

Brown v. Board of Education (1954), provides another example. The plaintiffs in *Brown* challenged the constitutionality of segregated education under the Fourteenth Amendment. It could be plausibly argued that if the question of the legality of segregated education had been presented to those who drafted and ratified that Amendment, they would have said that it did not forbid segregated education. Nevertheless, the decision striking down the practice is clearly correct; the holding that segregated education is inherently unequal is compelled by the *purpose* of the Fourteenth Amendment. That purpose, to simplify a fair amount, was to permit blacks to enter the life of the community, and to prevent any disfavored minority from ever being relegated to second-class citizenship. In 1868, when the Amendment was adopted, public education, especially in the South (the place of overwhelming concern to drafters and ratifiers alike), was not central to achieving these goals. The Amendment's backers were more concerned with achieving equal rights to make contracts, own property, and be safe from violence. As American society changed over the next century however, the relation between a public education and the achievement of the Amendment's purposes of integration and protection became self-evident. Thus, by the time of the *Brown* decision, the original purpose could be achieved only by a finding that segregated public education violated the Fourteenth Amendment.

The search for purpose, in other words, can reconcile the *goals* adopted by those who drafted the Constitution to the needs of the present. Of course, this method, like any method can be criticized (and because it is a centrist solution the attack can come from both originalists and living constitution theorists). An attack from the latter would emphasize that the use of original purpose would fetter the nation to long-outmoded values. An originalist, of course, would emphasize the malleability of the purpose analysis.

§ 6.9　A Concluding Word

This Chapter has not exhausted the possibilities of how a constitution should be interpreted. The literature on that topic is enormous, and the range of suggestions impressive. This discussion has attempted to lay out the arguments of the main debate—between originalism and living constitution; it has also attempted to give a flavor of the challenges judges face when called upon to resolve constitutional questions. That challenge is to decide cases in a principled manner; to select decision-making techniques that will apply to all similar cases; and, as a result, to enhance the predictability and accountability of judicial decision-making.

For two centuries constitutional decision-making has proceeded with a combination of methods. Open-ended interpretation has often taken place, but respect for language, context, and history has also been strong. Resolution of the debate over how the Constitution should be interpreted is difficult, but one fact must be made clear. Lack of resolution of that question has not kept the Court from playing a major and widely respected role in the growth of the Republic.

PART D
THE CONSTITUTION AND PRECEDENT

§ 6.10 The Rule of Lenity

Stare decisis is often said to play a special role in constitutional adjudication. The classic statement comes from Justice Brandeis in Burnet v. Coronado Oil & Gas Co. (1932) (dissenting):

Stare decisis is usually the wise policy, because in most matters it is more important that the applicable rule of law be settled than that it be settled right. This is commonly true even where the error is a matter of serious concern, provided correction can be had by legislation. But in cases involving the Federal Constitution, where correction through legislative action is practically impossible, this court has often overruled its earlier decisions.

Much can be said for a relaxed or lenient rule of constitutional *stare decisis*. The difficulty of over-turning a constitutional decision through the amendment process means that in practice only the Supreme Court can correct its errors; as a result, if the Court should adhere to a rigid form of *stare decisis,* bad law—perhaps disastrous law— could wreak havoc with litigants and even the welfare of the nation. One need only think of the separate-but-equal doctrine of Plessy v. Ferguson (1896), to recognize the danger inherent in a rigid rule of *stare decisis* in constitutional law.

A rule of lenity also is desirable for those who adhere to some form of originalism; the concern of originalists should be with the text and history, not with case law. A strong believer in originalism, in other words, must be concerned that respect for precedent does not lead to upholding law which has strayed from the framers' goals. As Justice Scalia, quoting from Justice Douglas, has written, the Justices swear to uphold the Constitution, "not the gloss which [the Court] may have put upon it." South Carolina v. Gathers (1989) (dissenting).

Of course, there is another side to the equation. *Stare decisis* plays a very important role in our law: it brings stability and predictability, it makes decision-making more efficient, and it provides for uniformity in decisions. These values have great significance in constitutional decision-making.

Stability is important because our fundamental law should not vary on a day-to-day basis. Justice

Roberts once wrote that Supreme Court decisions had been overruled so often that an opinion of the Court had come to resemble "a restricted railroad ticket, good for this day and train only." Smith v. Allwright (1944). An example from the Civil War era involved the question of what the government could define to be "legal tender." This is an issue of great importance; obviously, financial markets need to know what constitutes "legal tender." We cannot have paper currency legal today but not legal tomorrow. Nevertheless, the Court could not make up its mind. *Compare* Hepburn v. Griswold (1870) (it is unconstitutional to require United States notes to be accepted as legal tender in repayment of a debt contracted for before passage of the Act authorizing the notes as legal tender) *with* The Legal Tender Cases (1871) (overruling *Hepburn*). The value of predictability in constitutional law extends well beyond the needs of private citizens. It is of great importance, for example, that the police know when a search can be made without a warrant, and that Congress know the range of legislation that it may enact under the Commerce Clause.

Accountability, however, may be the most important value served by *stare decisis* in constitutional law. *Stare decisis*—adherence to what earlier courts have done—reduces judicial discretion; that is, it limits the ability of judges to act in unprincipled ways. *Stare decisis,* therefore, makes it easier to hold judges accountable for their work. Accountability, in turn, increases respect. The Justices impose their will on the states, on Congress, and on the President by virtue of the respect they command for their work. That respect would be greatly diminished if a decision were thought to be no more than one of Justice Roberts' "restricted railroad tickets."

Respect for precedent also helps to remind the Court that it must remember its institutional role in the development of the nation. Precedents, Justice Frankfurter once wrote in a dissent, reveal "the wisdom of this Court as an institution transcending the moment * * *." Green v. United States (1957).

§ 6.11 The Rule of Avoidance

One canon of constitutional decision-making has achieved widespread acceptance. This is the belief that constitutional decisions should be avoided if another method of decision is available. Thus, if a statute can reasonably be construed to avoid a constitutional issue, or if a case can be decided on common law grounds, the court should do so. This canon has an impeccable lineage for it can be traced back to Chief Justice Marshall's opinion in Marbury v. Madison (1803). It also makes good sense.

First, avoiding constitutional questions is also a good way of avoiding the difficulties of interpretation and *stare decisis* in constitutional law. If another way can be found to dispose of the case, then perhaps the constitutional question need never be decided. Second, the judicial power to review legislative and executive actions pits the court against those co-equal branches of government; that confrontation, therefore, should be avoided, if possible, and it may not take place if all other issues must be resolved before reaching the constitutional question.

As always, however, there are costs to consider. A judge eager to find a non-constitutional escape hatch might well force that result by engaging in a bad piece of statutory construction or fact-finding. (Ironically, Marshall is today commonly thought to have done the reverse in *Marbury*—he construed a statute badly and, therefore, had to *reach* the question of its constitutionality.) Another drawback is delay—deciding the non-constitutional issue first often will merely delay resolution of a constitutional problem. That delay harms the litigants, of course; and if the problem is a recurrent one, either for the litigants or for others, then delay may cause serious hardship.

One aspect of the rule of avoidance has become a well-known part of the abstention doctrine. In Railroad Com'n of Texas v. Pullman (1941), the Court held that when faced with a choice between a federal constitutional claim and uncertain state law, a federal court should, in certain circumstances, abstain from deciding the constitutional claim until the state courts have resolved the state law issue. If the state court resolves the case on the state law issue, the delay will permit the federal courts to avoid ruling on a constitutional question.

*

INDEX

———

References are to Pages

———

303

†